Let's TALK

Communication Skills and Conflict Transformation

with Leader's Guide

BARRY C. BARTEL

Herald
Press

Newton, Kansas
Winnipeg, Manitoba

Scottdale, Pennsylvania
Waterloo, Ontario

Printed in the United States of America.

International Standard Book Number 0-87303-340-X

Design by Gwen M. Stamm; Pontius Puddle cartoons by Joel Kauffmann; printing by Valley Offset Printing, Inc.

Unless otherwise noted, scripture text is from the New Revised Standard Version, copyright © 1989, Division of Christian Education of the National Council of the Churches of Christ in the United States of America.

Let's Talk: Communication Skills and Conflict Transformation is a revision and update of *Communication Skills and Conflict Resolution (student guide)* by Barry C. Bartel © 1983, Faith & Life Press.

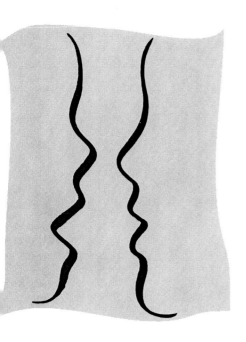

Contents

Foreword *by Ron Kraybill* 5

Introduction 7

How to Use this Book 8

1. What Is Your Conflict Management Style? 9
2. From Win/Lose to Win/Win 17
3. The Bible on Conflict 23
4. Honesty in Action 27
5. Speaking Without Words 33
6. Active Listening 37
7. Speaking with Care 45
8. What If the Other Person Is a Complete Idiot? . . 52
9. The Third Party and Conflict 59
10. Made in God's Image 65

Appendix A: Statement from the Mennonite Churches:
"Agreeing and Disagreeing in Love" 68
Appendix B: Bibliography 70
Leader's Guide 73

Foreword

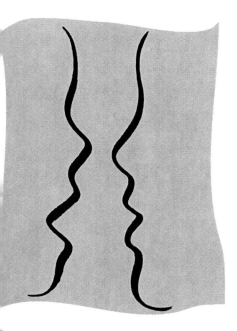

Be cautious. Seriously . . . you may become a different person if you enter fully into careful study of the material in this book. Few things change people and make them grow like conflict. I know, because my own life and relationships have deepened as I have struggled with conflict.

So what's so great about conflict? How do you grow when people are upset and hurt? Why not get away from the whole mess? That is what people were saying some time ago in a church torn by conflict. The parties involved were saying, "No point in trying to talk with *those* folks (the other party)." And people in the church who might have been mediators were saying, "That's not really our business." Eventually the conflict ended up in court.

One of my teachers, a man named Paul, was acquainted with this church. He was upset with the way the church handled things or rather *didn't* handle them. He sat down and wrote a rather angry letter about conflict, and why it's wrong to run from it. His words are recorded in 1 Corinthians 6:1-8.

What intrigues me is Paul's comment that "You will judge the angels and the world some day; therefore start right now with these trivial matters among yourselves. . . . Surely you have people among you wise enough to mediate" (my paraphrase). No room for shrugging off conflict here! We are to begin now with the same sort of things we will someday do in eternity. When we attempt to listen, to understand, and to make wise and fair decisions, we actually get a foretaste of eternity. We invite heaven down to earth.

That's one reason why you may end up a changed person if you commit yourself to the knowledge and skills contained in this booklet. When you talk about dealing with conflict, you're not just talking about nice ideas dreamed up by nice people. You're participating in a process that links you directly to eternity, that leads in the end to God.

Unfortunately, many Christians don't understand this. Better to avoid conflict, act as though it doesn't exist, or not let people with differing opinions speak, they think. The problem with this is that you can't make conflict go away just by pretending it is not there. Sooner or later you need to talk things through and sooner is usually easier than later. Besides, when you avoid differences, you lose a chance to learn and really think things through from all sides.

Maybe most importantly, when Christians run from conflict they run from taking an honest look at themselves. I have learned that the best times to see my own shadow side are when I am involved in conflict. That's because my ego, my selfishness, my desire to win even at the expense of others, my fear of looking like a fool or being rejected—all these shadowy things come slinking forward when I am in a conflict. No, I don't like the murky things I see when I am in conflict, but they are a part of me and I can't wish them away. What I've learned is that, as long as I look them in the face and acknowledge their existence, I can make better choices. I can consciously choose to follow Christ instead of being chased by the shadows.

The ability to choose is what makes the difference. When I choose to keep on listening in a disagreement, I am prepared for the appearance of the shadows. I know they are there and so I can choose not to be ruled by them. Thus I have found that my spiritual life deepens each time I choose to encounter the shadows. The brilliant presence of Christ easily overcomes darkness, but only when I choose to face the darkness.

So, yes, be cautious. If you are not interested in growth and change, this study is not for you. If you can't face what's inside of you, read no further. On the other hand, if you believe in life and hope and God, even where there are shadows, continue. This book may replace your caution with confidence.

—*Ron Kraybill, Associate Professor*
  at Eastern Mennonite University,
  Director of EMU Conflict Transformation Program

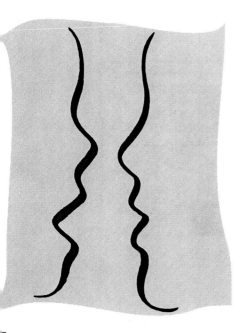

Introduction

I originally wrote this curriculum as a project for a class taught by Ron Kraybill in 1982 at Bethel College, North Newton, Kansas. Ron, and the Mennonite Conciliation Service that he directed at the time, have been pioneers in the study and application of conflict resolution methods. His influence and ideas pervade this study, originally published in 1983 as *Communication Skills and Conflict Resolution* (Newton, Kan.: Faith & Life Press, 1983). It presents only an introductory look at skills and issues involved in conflict management, primarily at the inter-personal level. As such, it is designed for adult and youth Sunday school classes, and other educational settings in the church.

Much has been written, studied, and practiced in the area of conflict management in the 15 years since this study was first published. I have been involved in many ways: through presenting workshops, helping individuals and groups work to manage disagreements, mediating conflicts through practicing law, and more recently in my work with Mennonite Central Committee in Bolivia. I have learned the most from my wife Brenda and our two children, Jordan and Leah.

Some of the concepts presented here may be familiar to you. I challenge you to take the material seriously, nevertheless. I often learn more as I present these materials in a workshop setting—by interacting with the ideas in a new group, and by refocusing my attention on skills that more practice can always improve. By becoming skilled with the ideas in this curriculum, you can model them for others and empower others to deal more effectively with conflict. These ideas also provide a springboard from which to assess whether church and other organizational structures and meetings foster effective communication and are a productive forum in which to deal with conflict. Workshops and training are available to help congregations and other organizations deal with these issues, and to intervene in crisis conflict management situations where necessary. (Also see page 70 for an annotated list of resources.)

—*Barry C. Bartel*

How to Use this Book

This manual is your workbook for a group learning experience in communication skills and conflict transformation. Each chapter includes important content on key communication and conflict management concepts, as well as individual and group exercises to help translate those concepts into positive habits. The book will also be a valuable reference as you perfect your skills long after the formal study is over.

It cannot be stressed enough that this kind of study is almost useless unless the learnings are practiced, and practiced again. The blanks for written answers need to be filled in. The role plays must be enacted, and the stories and biblical passages must be digested. Discussion and reflection on our life-journeys are crucial in bringing the concepts home. The more dog-eared this book can become in the learning experience, the greater the value you will get out of it.

If you are the facilitator or teacher of the group, you will find extra helps on page 73. We encourage you to become familiar with the whole study beforehand, so that you will know which parts will be particularly relevant to your group and may need extra planning or time.

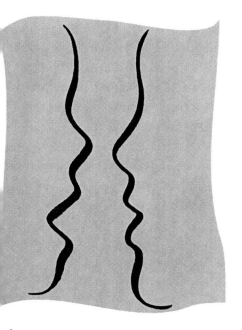

1

What Is Your Conflict Management Style?

Many different kinds of conflict surround us. We read about some, hear about some, and are directly involved in others. Think about the past several weeks. What conflicts come to mind? Make a list of conflicts you recall on the personal level, in your church or community, and at the national or international level.

_____	_____
_____	_____
_____	_____
_____	_____
_____	_____

There are different ways to respond to conflict. The following exercise gives you a basis for understanding your conflict management style. You may share your results with others if you like, or they can be kept confidential.

Exercise 1
Self-Assessment: Personal Response to Conflict*

Instructions: Read the description of each situation and the five possible responses listed after each. Circle the letter of the two responses you would most likely use in this situation.

1. You and another person, Jeremy, are co-leaders of a group. Together you are supposed to share the responsibilities of planning, organizing, and leading the group's activities and meetings. Jeremy has been getting very involved in other activities and has not been fulfilling his share of the duties, leaving you with much more responsibility. You, too, have obligations to other activities. Your pastor notices this and talks to you about the situation. In this situation, you would:

---

* Adapted from David W. Johnson, _Reaching Out: Interpersonal Effectiveness and Self-Actualization,_ Sixth Edition (Boston: Allyn and Bacon, 1997), pp. 40-44. Adapted by permission.]

a. Decide to talk to Jeremy, making it clear that you are unhappy with the situation, and that he must either begin doing his job or find a replacement.

b. Decide to talk to Jeremy, realizing that you have differing views on the situation. You suggest a compromise by which you give in some and expect the same of him.

c. You tell your pastor that you feel that Jeremy is doing a good enough job and that it's no big deal.

d. Decide to talk to Jeremy and find out why he is not fulfilling his duties, while making it clear that it bothers you. You tell him how you feel and listen to his reasons. Together, you try to solve the problem.

e. You approach Jeremy with your concerns, and he tells you that he is really busy with other obligations. Even though you are quite busy, too, you decide not to push the point so that you don't antagonize Jeremy. You adjust your schedule and continue to do most of the planning.

2. You and a friend, Jill, go to a lecture which has definite religious overtones. Afterwards, she asks you what your opinion is on the issues in the lecture. You tell her, and you discover that you agree on some issues, but disagree quite a bit on others. In this situation, you would:

f. Discuss the issues you disagree about, telling her how you feel, but listening carefully to what she says, too. You attempt to carefully work through your differences.

g. Discuss the issues you disagree about fairly quickly, concluding that you both have some good points and that an intermediate view is probably more accurate than either of yours is individually.

h. Tell her that you'd rather talk about it some other time, and ask her if she'd like to go bowling.

i. Argue with her on the issue you disagree about to convince her of the merits of your position.

j. Briefly discuss the issues. As soon as you see that Jill is strongly committed to her views, you admit that she's probably right and that you haven't given that much thought to those issues.

3. In the hall before a meeting, you and Joel have a short, yet heated, disagreement. It's time for the meeting to start, and you both attend, each still thinking that you were right. Afterwards, you see Joel coming toward you, apparently wishing to discuss the disagreement with you. As he approaches, you think:

k. "It's not nice for me to disagree with Joel. I think I'll tell him he probably is right, after all."

l. "Maybe if we each back down a little, we can work out a compromise, even if we still don't totally agree."

m. "This will be a good chance to hear what he was saying, and to state my views a little more clearly. Maybe we can work this out."

n. "Oh, here comes Joel. I wish we could forget about this whole thing. I'll try to look like I'm in a hurry, and maybe he'll leave me alone."

o. "Good, here comes Joel. Now I'll be able to show him that he was mistaken ."

4. When Joel reaches you, you would:

p. Tell him that you have to hurry to get somewhere or to talk to someone.

q. Try to show him that what you were saying really did make sense.

r. Suggest a middle position in the disagreement which requires both of you to give in a little bit.

s. Admit that you were probably wrong even though you may not have been, and apologize for upsetting him.

t. Sit down with him to discuss the disagreement, and try to solve the problem.

5. You are taking a computer class, and have weekly lab sessions. You and your partner, Erin, share the computer lab time, but must do separate work. Erin is clearly not being fair to you in her use of the assigned computer time. She almost acts as if she is the only one using the computer. In this situation, you would:

u. Request to talk to her about the use of the assigned computer time. Listen to her reasons for using it as she does, and try to work with her in solving the problem.

v. Tell her bluntly that she is being unfair to you. You quickly conclude that her excuses aren't adequate, and insist that she take more care in allowing you fair use of the computer.

w. Talk to her about the situation. When she explains her position, you suggest a solution which is better than what has been going on, but which still doesn't seem totally fair to you.

x. Mention the situation to her. She explains that she doesn't think she is being unfair, and you leave it at that.

y. Rather than risk a hassle, you try your best to work under the circumstances by planning your labs around hers, making a little more work for you than was intended by the instructor.

6. You work as a clerk at a local grocery store. You alternate working Saturdays with Ethan, so that you work the first and third Saturday of each month, and Ethan works the second and fourth Saturdays. The normal procedure for determining which of you works when there is a fifth Saturday is purely random; the boss flips a coin. It's the fourth Saturday and time to decide who will work the fifth Saturday. Both you and Ethan have something else planned for that Saturday: you are entered in a tennis tournament, and Ethan is planning to go out with his girlfriend. But someone needs to work. In this situation, you would:

A. Talk to Ethan and tell him how important this tennis tournament is to you. You listen to his reasons for wanting to go out. Together you try to work something out with the boss so neither of you has to work, though he may not allow that and may simply flip the coin.

B. Avoid all this trouble, and just accept the consequences of the coin flip.

C. Try to convince Ethan that he and his girlfriend can go to town anytime, but that your tennis tournament can only be played that Saturday.

D. Ask Ethan about his plans for Saturday, and when he explains that he and his girlfriend have the whole day planned, you agree that they can go ahead and go to town, and that you'll just wait for the next tournament.

E. Tell Ethan how important this tournament is to you, and suggest that you could work between your 7:00 a.m. match and your 2:00 p.m. match if Ethan could go to town then and work the rest of the afternoon.

7. You need to replace a failed component on your computer. You go to a computer store and correctly describe the replacement part you need. The store doesn't have the exact component you requested, but the sales clerk recommends another brand, saying it will work as well as or better than the component you requested. The store has a no-refund/no-exchange policy on electronic parts that have been installed. When you install the component, you discover it is not fully compatible with your computer and causes the computer to perform certain functions more slowly. In this situation, you would:

F. Go back to the store and explain the problem. You listen to their explanation of the excuse, and explain your position to try to resolve the problem.

G. Go back to the store and explain the situation. You acknowledge their no-exchange policy, and suggest a 50% refund.

H. Call your spouse or friend, explain the situation, and ask whether he or she could take the component back and try to get a refund.

I. Take the part back and explain the situation. When they explain that the part works when installed properly, you accept the blame and put up with the inconvenience of the slower part.

J. Take the part back to the store and, despite their no-exchange policy, explain the situation and demand that they give you a refund for the incompatible part.

8. Someone is bothered by something you have done, and asks to talk to you about it. How would you react to this situation?

K. You feel as if she is causing unnecessary tension, and wish she wouldn't pursue the issue very far.

L. You apologize for the fact that it is bothering her, and tell her you'll try to work on it so that it doesn't bother her anymore.

M. You're sorry that this bothers her, but since it does, you're glad she brought it up. You listen carefully to her and deal with her criticism.

N. You defend your actions and explain to the other person how her complaints aren't warranted.

O. You don't really agree that she has a legitimate complaint, but since it bothers her, you try to compromise so that you are both satisfied with the result.

9. Think of a conflict in the last few weeks in which you were one of the conflicting parties. How did you deal with that conflict?

P. Agreed to give in on some points if the other person gave in on some points in order to find a compromise.

Q. Postponed the discussion, or tried to get away from it with as little tension as possible.

R. Argued with the other person (or persons) to demonstrate how your position was correct.

S. Tried to get all the issues out and work through differences.

T. Tried not to hurt the other person's feelings, even to the point of agreeing to do something you would really rather not do.

10. In general, how do you deal with conflict?

U. Approach a conflict with the feeling that you have the right to voice your position and to hear the other person's position, and that somehow you'll be able to find a solution which satisfies both of you.

V. Try to convince the other person of the merits of your position, and pursue your goals as long as you think you are right.

W. Try to avoid useless tension and unpleasantness; try to stay away from conflict and the difficulties it often creates.

X. Try to find a fair compromise with the other person, which consists of gains and losses for both of you.

Y. Sacrifice your own wishes to soothe other people's feelings; be considerate of others and try to make them happy.

After you have circled two responses for each of these situations, turn to the chart on the next page. At the top, there is a row entitled "Your Responses." Now go back through your responses. Circle the letters on this chart which coincide with your responses. Note that upper and lower case letters represent different responses.

When you have completed this, add the number of letters you have circled in each column, and put that number in the box provided in each column. If one column has a much larger number in it than the others, that is likely the predominant way you deal with conflict. You may want to plot your position on the graph on page 16.

For Discussion/Reflection

• How do most people you know deal with conflict? Do you have more respect or less respect for people who respond to conflict in certain ways than for others?
• Why is it difficult or uncomfortable to deal with conflict?
• Do you agree or disagree that, as the chart suggests, avoiding conflict shows a low commitment to a relationship? Why?
• Does anything about the chart surprise you? Are there items on the chart with which you disagree or which you feel are particularly insightful?

For Your Personal Reflection

What is your normal response to conflict, according to this exercise? Do you feel comfortable with that conclusion? Do you agree with the assessment? How do you wish you would normally respond to conflict?

For Next Time

Think about how Jesus responded to conflict. Was he aggressive, or did he stay away from conflict? Skim the Gospels of Matthew, Mark, Luke, and John, and find some examples of how Jesus dealt with conflict. Bring a Bible to the next session. Read the first several pages of Chapter 2 before coming to the next meeting.

Determining Your Conflict Management Style—Response Chart

Responses	a i o q v C J N R V	d f m t u A F M S U	b g l r w E G O P X	c h n p y B H K Q W	e j k s x D I L T Y
Conflict Management Type	Competitive "The Shark"	Collaborative "The Owl"	Sharing "The Fox"	Avoiding "The Turtle"	Accommodating "The Teddy Bear"
Commitment to Personal Goals	High	High	Medium	Low	Low
Commitment to Relationships	Low	High	Medium	Low	High
Additional Comments	"The Shark" forces others to accept his or her way. Oblivious to needs or feelings of others. Believes conflicts are settled by one person losing. The Shark wants to win and will fight at any cost to do so. While you're talking, the Shark is thinking of his or her next argument to defeat you.	"The Owl" confronts openly and fairly. Optimistic about conflict. Committed to personal goals and to other's goals. Begins discussions by identifying openly the wishes of both. Never satisfied until a solution is found that satisfies both. "If we just keep working at this we'll find a way for both of us." When the Owl talks, he or she may come on strong, but when you talk, the Owl is listening carefully and sympathetically.	"The Fox" compromises. Gives up some goals if you'll give up some of yours. Similar to the Owl, but less optimistic about conflict bringing an improved relationship. When the Fox is talking, he or she is diplomatic but persuasive. When you talk, the Fox is trying hard to figure out some compromise.	"The Turtle" withdraws. Believes it is hopeless to try to resolve conflict. Avoids people and issues that may cause conflict. Feels helpless to gain his goals and refuses to cooperate with others in gaining theirs. The Turtle neither talks nor listens. You won't even get a chance to discuss things with the Turtle.	"The Teddy Bear" soothes. More than anything else, Teddy Bear wants others to accept him or her. Quick to accommodate to others and ignore own needs because the Teddy Bear believes that asking others to meet his or her needs will harm the relationship. When the Teddy Bear talks, everything sounds just fine. When you talk he or she is listening and agreeing with everything you say.

*The original version of the chart "Responses to Conflict" was compiled by Ron Kraybill, with reference to the second edition of David W. Johnson's *Reaching Out: Interpersonal Effectiveness and Self-Actualization.*

Conflict Management Styles

From your responses on page 15, determine where your conflict management style falls in the following graph.

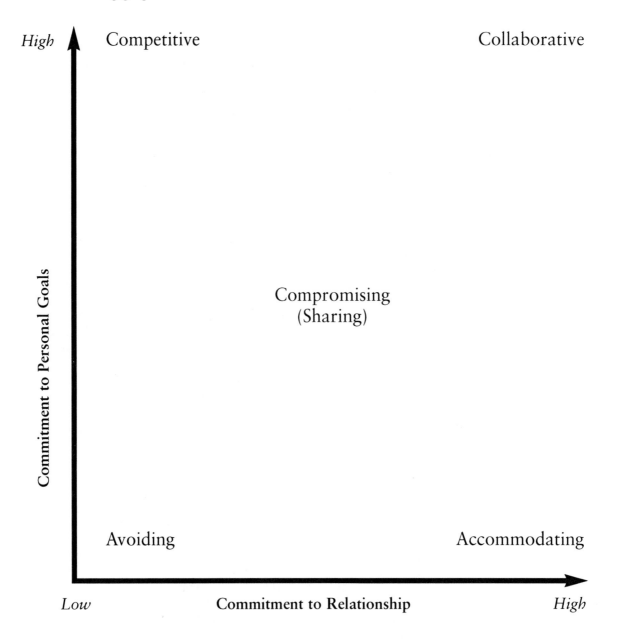

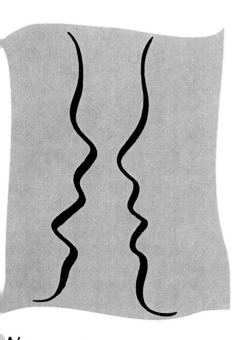

2

From Win/Lose to Win/Win

When you think of conflict, what do you think of? List some synonyms for the word *conflict*. Also list several adjectives (words and phrases) that you would use to describe conflict.

_____   _____
_____   _____
_____   _____
_____   _____
_____   _____

Conflict Avoidance

Often the word *conflict* carries negative overtones. We think of it as something bad. People sometimes assume that the best way to make peace is to avoid dealing with conflict. The Scriptures, however, present peacemaking not as passive avoidance, but active reconciliation. Since we aren't all the same, conflict is an inevitable part of everyone's life. To deny the existence of conflict in our everyday life is to deny reality, yet many people continue to do so, or avoid dealing with the conflict that does exist. It often seems that it is easier to run from conflict than to face it. A more positive, long-range view of conflict will reveal a side of conflict that is often neglected.

For Discussion/Reflection

Why do many people have a negative view of conflict? What is your response to the attitude that the best way to make peace is to avoid conflict? Are there situations where the best response is to avoid dealing with a conflict? Think of someone who continually avoids dealing with conflict, and think of some specific incidents where conflict was avoided. What happened in these specific examples?

Consider this scenario:
A group of eight high school students went to a three-week music camp one summer. Kristen and Katie, good friends from school, roomed together during the camp.

Kristen would often get upset that Katie played her music too loudly, or had friends in their room too much. But rather than telling Katie what bothered her, Kristen would ignore it or go to a friend's room. So everything seemed all right.

This went on for two weeks. Then one day Kristen was reading in their room, and Katie brought some friends in and turned on the stereo. Finally, Kristen just couldn't take it. She jumped up, screamed at Katie, and stormed out of the room.

Katie was surprised and felt terrible. The next day Kristen apologized to Katie and explained that she didn't know what had gotten into her.

What happened in this example? Why? Kristen was avoiding conflict in a series of incidents. She was afraid to confront Katie and tell her how she felt; instead, she suppressed her feelings. What was the result? What effect did it have on Kristen's relationship with Katie? Was Kristen being fair to Katie by not confronting her? Why or why not?

Effects of Avoidance

Avoidance of conflict often has two results:

1. Unnecessary blowups over minor issues
2. Cooling of relationships

Both of these results were present in the example of Kristen and Katie. If Kristen would have told Katie from the start that the music bothered her, Katie would have known that Kristen was irritated and likely would have turned down the volume. Continual avoidance of the conflict finally resulted in an explosion of hard feelings. So, in trying to keep from hurting the relationship, Kristen actually made things worse by avoiding the conflict.

You have probably been in situations where someone gets very upset over something very minor, and then "doesn't know what came over them." When people suppress hard feelings rather than dealing with them when they develop, those feelings keep growing inside. Eventually, they need to be vented. Some people vent them by hitting something, jogging, or listening to loud music. But often, venting the emotion without dealing with the cause of the emotion (hard feelings toward someone) is not enough. The emotions may begin to pile up inside again. For many people, these suppressed

Pontius' Puddle

feelings eventually get vented by blowing up when something minor irritates them. This is unfair to everyone involved.

But even venting emotions by blowing up at someone does not take care of the original cause of the hard feelings. Those hard feelings can easily get in the way of a close or casual friendship. A degree of closeness is sacrificed by trying to avoid conflict. Avoiding the conflict can lead to avoiding the person. This is not a healthy way to maintain friendships. This is ironic, because people who avoid conflict often do so because they think it's the best way to keep from hurting a relationship!

In the short run, not dealing with conflict may seem to preserve a relationship. But in the long run, the relationship does get hurt. Refer to the graph on page 16. Notice that failure to deal with conflict shows a low commitment to personal goals and to relationships. Avoiding a conflict suggests that you don't care enough about yourself or about your relationship with someone else to risk a little tension by approaching that person.

For Discussion/Reflection

Have you ever seen avoidance of conflict in the church? Why was conflict not dealt with? What happened? Have you seen situations in which failure to deal with conflict led to a blowup over a minor incident, or where the closeness of a relationship was sacrificed?

Another Way

A college professor tells of a situation he encountered in one of his classes. A group of students usually sat in the back row of the room and passed notes back and forth during the lecture. The students were not being obnoxious, but the note-passing bothered the professor and distracted him from his lecture. After this had happened a few times, the professor asked to talk to the students after class. He told them that he had noticed them passing notes during his lectures, and that it distracted him and made it difficult for him to concentrate on his lectures. He asked them if they would please stop passing notes. The students apologized and said that they did not realize they were distracting him, and that they did not intend to cause any disturbance. The note-passing stopped.

The professor could have gone through the semester without saying anything to the students. He could have continued to suppress his annoyance with the students, and likely would have gotten more and more irritated with the students as the semester went on. The students didn't even realize that they were distracting the professor, but an unhealthy wall between them might have formed. Confronting the students stopped the note-passing and made the professor more comfortable delivering his lectures. The professor was fair to the students and fair to himself.

The Case for Avoidance

In most cases, avoidance is not the most appropriate response to conflict. This does not mean, though, that conflict should never be avoided.

Consider this example:

You pull out of a parking lot onto the street. You accidentally cut in front of another driver who is forced to slow down for you. At the next intersection, he pulls up next to your car, shaking his fist and yelling obscene things at you.

There is definitely a conflict here between you and the other driver. Avoidance may be the most appropriate response. But why? The critical aspect of this example, which makes avoidance appropriate, is that there is no relationship to preserve. There is no risk of a blowup over a future issue if you don't know the person, and there is no relationship that can "grow cold."

Why is conflict avoidance such a common response? It has a lot to do with the way we look at conflict. Our culture has taught us that conflict is a win/lose situation, that in a conflict, one person or group will win, and the other will lose. We even carry this attitude to interpersonal conflicts and, as a result, often avoid conflict because of the risk of "losing."

It is more healthy to approach conflict as a win/win situation. It is not necessary in a conflict for one side to win and the other to lose. In fact, the graph on page 16 shows that resolving conflict (collaborating or sharing) shows a high or medium commitment to a relationship, as well as to personal goals. In other words, resolving conflict rather than avoiding it makes conflict a win/win situation (the relationship, as well as personal goals, are strengthened). Both parties in a conflict gain from its resolution.

Conflict as a Win/Win Situation

Conflict is a mark of involvement. Conflicting parties must have a degree of involvement with each other. Emotion in conflict shows a high level of commitment and caring.

Conflict clarifies ideas. By bringing conflict issues out in the open, the issues are clarified, and better ideas can be generated.

Conflict helps define identity. By working through conflict, people gain a better understanding of themselves, and others get a clearer understanding of them.

Conflict stimulates creativity. Faced with challenging conflict situations, people must think creatively of new ways to deal with problems.

Conflict opens a potential for new and deeper relationships. Working through, rather than avoiding conflict, strengthens relationships.

Conflict binds people together. A strong binding force develops between people who can successfully work through conflicts.

For Discussion/Reflection

Do you agree that these items can make dealing with conflict a win/win situation? What other positive things can happen if conflict is dealt with effectively? In your experience, do conflicts usually get "resolved"? How often are conflicts simply "managed"? What would it mean to "transform" conflict into a positive experience?

Jesus' Response to Conflict

By nature of his position and personality, Jesus was often in conflict situations. Read the following descriptions of Jesus in conflict situations:

- Matthew 19:16-30 (parallel passages: Mark 10:17-31, and Luke 18:18-30)
- Matthew 13:53-58 (parallel passages: Mark 6:1-6, and Luke 4:16-30)
- John 10:22-42
- Luke 4:16-30, John 8:59, 10:39, 11:45-57
- Mark 11:15-19
- Matthew 23:13-28 (parallel passages: Mark 12:40, Luke 11:39-42, 44, 52; 20:47)
- John 10:32 and 18:32
- Matthew 19:16-30 (parallel passages: Mark 10:17-31, Luke 18:18-30)

For Discussion/Reflection

What did you conclude from your reading and thinking about Jesus' response to conflict? Was Jesus' response predominantly accommodating? Did he avoid conflict? Or was his response more competitive and collaborative?

We, like Jesus, need to openly deal with conflict to realize the long-term benefits of strengthened relationships and to feel better about ourselves. Jesus' life exemplifies this challenge.

Tale of Two Churches

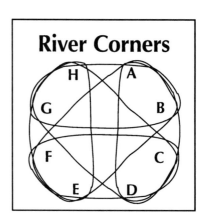

River Corners Congregation is experiencing conflict. Should they add a new wing to the sanctuary? Several subgroups (A, B, C and D) say yes. They are spending time together, preparing a convincing case for why the group needs a new sanctuary. Other subgroups (E, F, G and H) disagree. They are preparing reasons why the money should go to mission programs.

There's more conflict at this little outpost of the peaceable kingdom. Should they include contemporary music in worship? Some members (G, H, A and B) say yes. Other (C, D, E and F) have been working together to show that the old traditions are still best.

There's a third conflict. Local demonstrations against nuclear weapons have been controversial. Several members (A, B, E and F) recently asked the congregation to house the office of a local disarmament group. Other members (C. D, G and H) got red in the face just hearing about this request. They're meeting to outline reasons to shoot it down.

There are other conflicts. Some love the pastor, others don't. Some support the local denominational college, others don't.

If you were looking for a place to worship, would you be interested?

Now look at another congregation, Placid Grove. This group also has conflict over a building program. Some members are for it, A, B, C and D); some against it (E, F, G and H). They have conflict over contemporary music—some support it but others are opposed. Some support the nuclear freeze; others are opposed. Some love the pastor, some do not. Some support the denominational college, others do not.

Placid Grove

Now which congregation would you rather join?

From the standpoint of conflict management, the first congregation, River Corners, is healthy. No conflict could split this group. Rather, every issue provides opportunity for members to cooperate with different people. The result is a "cross-stitching" effect which binds the group together in diverse alliances. At Placid Grove, in contrast, conflict divides. Each issue only deepens the gulf between two groups who communicate rarely and poorly. Any emotional issue could paralyze and split the church.*

For Discussion/Reflection

In 1995 the Mennonite Church and the General Conference Mennonite Church adopted the statement "Agreeing and Disagreeing in Love," reprinted as Appendix A on page 68. Review the statement. What attitude toward conflict does it represent? Which congregation in "The Tale of Two Churches" is more likely to have applied the statement's principles?

Unity

based on Philippians 2:1-8:

Jesus, help us live in peace,
From our blindness set us free.
Fill us with your healing love.
Help us live in unity.

Many times we disagree
O'er what's right or wrong to do.
It's so hard to really see
From the other's point of view.

How we long for pow'r and fame,
Seeking ev'ry earthly thing.
We forget the One who came
As a Servant not a king.

© 1971 by Gerald Derstine. From the *Sing and Rejoice* songbook (Scottdale, Pa.: Herald Press, 1979). Used with permission.

---

* From the fall 1997 issue of the Mennonite Conciliation Service Quarterly. Used by permission.

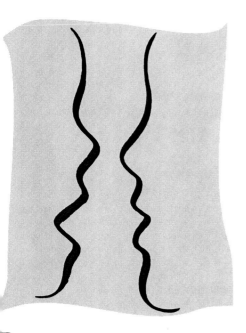

3

The Bible on Conflict

Be angry but do not sin; do not let the sun go down on your anger (Ephesians 4:26).

The response to anger, disagreement, and conflict in Christian settings is often that conflict is not a "Christian" activity. People may feel that it is a sin to disagree, that disagreement shows a lack of love. Let's examine those ideas from a biblical perspective. Ephesians 4:26 says it is not a sin to *be* angry, but rather, that we should not *stay* angry.

For Discussion/Reflection

What does it mean to "not let the sun go down on your anger?" How can anger lead to sin? Is conflict *always* sin? Is conflict *ever* sin? Why or why not? What is your reaction to the following statement made in the midst of a congregational meeting: "If we were really Christians, we wouldn't be disagreeing like this!" What is your response to the attitude that the church which invites open expression of disagreement will have less conflict?

Conflict in the Bible

A number of places in the Bible speak specifically to the theme of conflict resolution. The concern of these passages is not whether or not there *should* be conflict; it is assumed that conflict will exist. Rather the concern of the biblical references is how to *deal* with conflict.

You shall not hate in your heart anyone of your kin; you shall reprove your neighbor, or you will incur guilt yourself. You shall not take vengeance or bear a grudge against any of your people, but you shall love your neighbor as yourself: I am the Lord (Leviticus 19:17, 18).

This passage advocates the settling of differences rather than avoiding conflict. Interestingly, verse 17 suggests that it can be a sin if you *don't* resolve the differences. In other words, if not resolving differences leads to hard feelings, revenge, or hate, it is sin. But the conflict itself is not sin. By settling the differences, you show that you love your neighbor as you love yourself.

Come to terms quickly with your accuser while you are on the way to court with him (Matthew 5:25a).

Matthew says that if there is a dispute, you should settle it before taking it to court. The conflict should be settled on a personal basis between the individuals. The conflict itself is not seen as wrong.

So when you are offering your gift at the altar, if you remember that your brother or sister has something against you, leave your gift there before the altar and go; first be reconciled to your brother and sister, and then come and offer your gift (Matthew 5:23, 24).

Matthew says that if you have a dispute with your brother or sister, you should go settle it. The dispute itself is not bad, but if it is not settled, it comes between God and you. When you make peace with your brother or sister, your relationship with God can be set right.

I urge Euodia and I urge Syntyche to be of the same mind in the Lord. Yes, and I ask you also, my loyal companion, help these women, for they have struggled beside me in the work of the gospel, together with Clement and the rest of my co-workers, whose names are in the book of life (Philippians 4:2,3).

Paul does not condemn the women for having a disagreement. He does not suggest that the two women avoid the conflict and leave. Rather, he tells them to work to reach an agreement. He even asks others to help the two women reach an agreement. In fact, Paul puts as much responsibility for resolving the disagreement on the others as he does on the women themselves.

 ## For Discussion/Reflection

What teachings do you feel are most important from the Scriptures quoted above? Do you agree that the concern of the Scriptures is not whether there is conflict, but how we deal with it? Why or why not? What other Scriptures support your view? Please refer to the statement "Agreeing and Disagreeing in Love" (page 68) for further biblical reflection.

Procedure in Matthew 18

The Gospel according to Matthew gives a description of the successive steps to take in dealing with a conflict that has resulted in sin:

If another member of the church sins against you, go and point out the fault when the two of you are alone. If the member listens to you, you have regained that one. But if you are not listened to, take one or two others along with you, so that every word may be confirmed by the evidence of two or three witnesses. If the member refuses to listen to them, tell it to the church; and if the offender refuses to listen even to the church, let such a one be to you as a Gentile and a tax collector.

ruly I tell you, whatever you bind on earth will be bound in heaven, and whatever ou loose on earth will be loosed in heaven.

Again, truly I tell you, if two of you agree on earth about anything you ask, it will be 'one for you by my Father in heaven. For where two or three are gathered in my ame, I am there among them. (Matthew 18:15-20)

For Discussion/Reflection

Have you seen this process at work? What were the results? Review and discuss this Scripture line by line. Are conflict and sin the same thing? Always? Sometimes? Never? Why is the first step private? Why does the second step involve taking one or two others? Why tell the whole thing to the church? What does it mean to treat the person as a pagan or a tax collector? Consider Matthew 9:13, in which Jesus says that "I have come to call not the righteous but sinners."

What does Matthew 18:15-20 say about the importance of dealing with conflict in the context of the church? How important is reconciliation to the life of the church? What does verse 20 say about the presence of God in the process of dealing with conflict?

Many Gifts

By speaking the truth in love, we must grow up in every way into him who is the head, nto Christ, from whom the whole body, joined and knit together by every ligament vith which it is equipped, as each part is working properly, promotes the body's rowth in building itself up in love. (Ephesians 4:15,16)

*J*ust as the body is a combination of different parts, the church is composed of a group of individuals, each with different skills and gifts. But they must all work together to *be* a church, just as all parts of the body must work together. Just as there is no church without individuality (diversity), there is no church without disagreement. These different views must be expressed in a spirit of love.

At one congregational meeting, there was a strong disagreement. One member stood *up* in the middle and proclaimed that they were not loving since they were disagreeing. *Quite* the contrary! It is precisely by disagreeing in a spirit of love that commitment and caring are expressed and, through this disagreement, the church grows and is strengthened.

For Discussion/Reflection

What do Jesus' teachings about turning the other cheek say about dealing with conflict? They are found in Matthew 5:38-40 and Luke 6:27, 28. Is this a call to avoid conflict? Is turning the other cheek a "fight" response? A "flight" response? Another type of response? Is it active or passive? Does it show weakness or strength? Consider the passage in John 18:19-24 in which Jesus was struck on the cheek.

For Discussion/Reflection

What do Jesus' teachings on forgiveness say about dealing with conflict? Review Matthew 18:21, 22, where Jesus says to forgive "seventy times seven" times. Note that this passage is a continuation of the passage from Matthew 18 quoted and studied above. What does that suggest about forgiveness? Consider also Ephesians 4:31, 32, Luke 17:3, 4, and other passages. Is forgiveness an active process or a passive event? Who is involved? Must anything happen before forgiveness can occur? Why or why not?

Adding It All Up

Conflict is very present both in our society and in the biblical record. A recurring theme in the New Testament is that conflict can be a process that strengthens relationships and commitments—and not an evil which should be avoided. Our concern should not be whether to deal with conflict, but how to deal with it. The following chapters provide guidance for approaching conflict in a healthy way.

Many Gifts

(based on I Corinthians 12)

There are many gifts, but the same Spirit.
There are many works, but the same God.
And the Spirit gives each as it chooses.
Praise the Lord. Praise God.

Now one has a gift of wisdom;
Another the calling to speak.
One the ability to comfort;
Another the calling to teach.

A body has many members,
Yet all work in unity.
The church is the body of Christ:
His arms, ears, and eyes, hands and feet.

Not all are called to be prophets;
And not all are called to preach.
But all should aim for the best gifts
And love is the greatest of these.

© 1977 by Patricia Shelly, used by permission.
The music is available in *Hymnal: A Worship Book*
(Newton, Kan.: Faith and Life Press; Elgin, Ill.: Brethren Press;
Scottdale, Pa.: Mennonite Publishing House; 1992), no. 304.

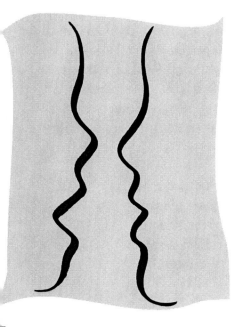

4
Honesty in Action

In Chapter 1 we identified five types of responses to conflict: competitive, collaborative, sharing, avoiding and accommodating. Another way in which responses to conflict are distinguished is in terms of submissiveness, assertiveness, and aggressiveness. Write down several words or phrases which you associate with these three terms:

Submissiveness	Assertiveness	Aggressiveness

For Discussion/Reflection

For which response did you write the most positive words and phrases? How are these categories like or unlike the five responses in Chapter 1 (competitive, collaborative, sharing, avoiding, accommodating)?

Defining Submissive, Assertive, Aggressive*

The following is an attempt to define the terms introduced above. As we go through the material, feel free to dialogue with the definitions, compare them with your word associations above, and reflect again on the way you tend to behave in a conflict situation.

Submissive behavior is that type of interpersonal behavior in which one complies with the needs of others and fails to stand up for one's own rights. One may fail to directly express one's true feelings, emotions, or opinions, but will allow others to decide or direct one's actions.

---

* The definitions of submissive, assertive, and aggressive behavior, along with the "Assertive Bill of Rights," were adapted from Sharon B. Molten, "Understanding Assertive Behavior," *MCC Peace Section Task Force on Women in Church and Society* (Akron, Pa.: Mennonite Central Committee, September-October, 1980), p. 3.

Note: This kind of passive submissiveness must be distinguished from the radical submission that the Bible calls us to live out, in which a person voluntary gives up his or her rights in service to another. The latter is an act of love, rooted in a strong sense of one's own self and one's rights—not one of powerlessness, nor a response to intimidation. Jesus' death on the cross is a supreme example of this life-giving "submission." This is what the apostle Paul has in mind when he instructs us to "be subject to one another out of reverence for Christ" (Ephesians 5:21).

Aggressive behavior is the type of behavior in which a person stands up for his or her own rights in such a way that the rights of others are violated. The purpose of aggressive behavior is to humiliate, dominate, or put the other person down, rather than to simply express one's honest emotions or thoughts. It is an attack on the other person rather than on the other person's behavior. It is often an overreaction or outburst.

Assertive behavior is interpersonal behavior in which a person stands up for his or her legitimate rights in such a way that the rights of others are not violated. Assertive behavior is an honest, direct, and appropriate expression of one's feelings, beliefs, and opinions. It communicates respect for the other person, although not necessarily for that person's behavior.

Submissive behavior does not fit well with the biblical view of conflict in Chapter 3, where we are told to settle our differences. Settling our differences doesn't involve passive submission, but an active attempt to work through differences and conflict. Submissiveness is very similar to avoidance.

Aggressive behavior, on the other hand, attempts to resolve conflict by running over the rights and feelings of others. This is not compatible with the Christian ethic of love: "Love your neighbor as yourself" (Matt. 22:39 and elsewhere), and "Love your enemies, do good to those who hate you, bless those who curse you, pray for those who abuse you" (Luke 6:27, 28).

Love for others mandates respecting their rights and feelings, but it does not mean bowing to their every need and desire. Assertiveness bridges the gap between the two extremes of submissiveness and aggressiveness.

Assertiveness involves being honest about your feelings to other people *and* being honest about them to yourself. It shows respect for *yourself* and for *others*. Honesty is the aspect of assertiveness that we will concentrate on.

Pontius' Puddle

Assertive Bill of Rights

You have the right to do what you desire as long as it doesn't hurt someone else.
You have the right to maintain dignity, even if it does hurt someone else.
You have the right to make a request of another person as long as you realize the other
  person has the right to say no.
You have the right to clarify and discuss problems with the persons involved.
You have the right to be treated with respect.
You have the right to have and express your own feelings.
You have the right to be listened to and taken seriously.
You have the right to set your own priorities.
You have the right to say no without feeling guilty or selfish.
You have the right to ask for what you want.
You have the right to get what you pay for.
You have the right to ask for information from professionals.
You have the right to make mistakes.
You have the right to choose not to assert yourself.

What is your response to this list? How do they square with biblical principles? Are
there other rights you would add?

Exercise 1

Assertive and Aggressive

The following scenarios call for a conflict response. Write both an aggressive and an
assertive response to each situation. The first one offers examples.

1. Your neighbors have a large dog which they keep in a small fenced area on the op-
   posite side of their backyard. There is no physical boundary between your property
   and theirs. They like to allow their dog to run free for an hour or so every day. Recently, it has been coming onto your property and digging in your garden, where it
   has killed a number of plants. You call your neighbors to tell them of the situation.

   Assertive Response
   I've noticed that you've been letting
   your dog run free occasionally.
   Recently he has been digging in my
   garden, and has killed several of my
   plants. Could we work out an arrange-
   ment so that the dog is not able to
   run free on my yard and garden?

   Aggressive Response
   Your stupid dog has ruined my garden!
   I knew from the beginning that you were
   too irresponsible to keep him under con-
   trol. If he ever comes on my property
   again, I'm calling the dog catcher.

2. You live near the local high school. A group of students walks by your house on
   the way to and from school every day. They have started taking a shortcut over
   the corner of your yard, and a trail has developed which is starting to kill the
   grass. You see the students on their way home from school one day and go out to
   confront them:

Assertive Response   Aggressive Response

_____   _____
_____   _____
_____   _____
_____   _____
_____   _____
_____   _____

3. You have been standing in line to be checked out at a grocery store for a long
    time. A person walks up and, not realizing that the line extended for quite a dis-
    tance, cuts in front of you. You tell the person:

Assertive Response   Aggressive Response

_____   _____
_____   _____
_____   _____
_____   _____
_____   _____
_____   _____

4. You took a kitchen appliance to a man to be repaired. You need the appliance fair
    ly regularly, and the man said that he would get to it right away and have it ready
    in a day or so. After waiting more than a week, the man has still not begun to
    work on the appliance. You tell him:

Assertive Response   Aggressive Response

_____   _____
_____   _____
_____   _____
_____   _____
_____   _____
_____   _____

5. You loaned your card table and some chairs to some friends several weeks ago.
    They said that they would return them a week after they borrowed them, but quite
    often they do not return things promptly. You need the card table and chairs in
    two days when you plan to have guests over. You call the friends who borrowed
    the table and chairs and say:

Assertive Response   Aggressive Response

_____   _____
_____   _____
_____   _____
_____   _____
_____   _____
_____   _____

For Discussion/Reflection

How are assertiveness, aggressiveness, and submissiveness like or unlike the five types of responses identified in Session 1 (competitive, collaborative, sharing, avoiding, and accommodating)? Tell stories in your group that illustrate how you have responded to conflict in submissive, aggressive, or assertive ways.

The Bible on Telling the Truth

So then, putting away falsehood, let all of us speak the truth to our neighbors, for we are members of one another. Be angry but do not sin; do not let the sun go down on your anger (Ephesians 4:25, 26).

Come, O children, listen to me; I will teach you the fear of the Lord. Which of you desires life, and covets many days to enjoy good? Keep your tongue from evil, and your lips from speaking deceit. Depart from evil, and do good; seek peace, and pursue it (Psalm 34:11-14).

Paul and the psalmist set the Christian stage for honesty. Paul's message is in the context of anger. He asks Christians not to stay angry all day, but rather to be honest about feelings and resolve them. The psalmist, too, rejects lying. Being honest and open about your feelings will make you much happier.

Honesty involves much more than just not lying. As Paul said, it involves *telling* the truth. It is an active expression of one's inner feelings. As a Christian response, it involves telling the truth without running over the rights and feelings of others. We have already seen the frustration of avoiding conflict and keeping hard feelings bottled up inside. Not being honest about your feelings teaches others to disregard your feelings and to mistreat you.

Being honest about your feelings is much less frustrating. Honesty shows respect for others and for yourself, and gains the respect of others. Honesty allows new relationships to form and strengthens existing relationships, making them more authentic and satisfying. And being honest about your feelings *now* makes it easier to be honest about your feelings in the future.

Just as Jesus cared enough about other people and their relationships with him to confront them openly and honestly, we should care enough to be open and honest. Truly

🍂 Pontius' Puddle

being honest about one's feelings can be uncomfortable; it's not easy to tell someone that something he or she does bothers you. But the development of any skill takes practice. In the long run, being honest makes situations more comfortable.

Exercise 2
Concordance Search

Consider how often the word "truth" is used in the Bible. Use a concordance to determine how often it is used. In what ways is the word used? When it refers to God (I Timothy 3:15), the Word (Galatians 2:14), and Jesus (John 14:6), is its meaning different than in Ephesians 4:15? How?

For Discussion/Reflection

What does it mean to tell the truth? Is it enough just not to lie? Is lying always wrong? What does it mean that "the truth hurts?" What does it mean in Ephesians 4:15 to "speak the truth in love?"

For Discussion/Reflection

Compare the Assertive Bill of Rights (see page 29) to Paul's lists of virtues in Galatians 5:22-23, Ephesians 4:2, Philippians 4:8, and I Timothy 6:11. Is there tension between the lists? Compare it also to what you learned in Chapter 2 about Jesus' personality and response to conflict.

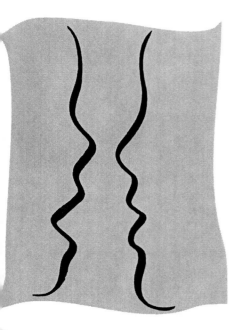

5

Speaking Without Words

Society uses many symbols. Flags represent countries, the cross symbolizes the crucifixion of Jesus, and two arms extended at full length above the head represents a touchdown or field goal. A heart means love, and the picture of a tent on a road sign indicates campsite.

Words are what many think of as the whole of communication. Our lifestyle and the nature of our society depend on the use of written and spoken language. But there is much more involved in communication than written and spoken language. In a normal conversation, the verbal components carry less than 35 percent of the social meaning of the situation, while more than 65 percent is carried by nonverbal messages.*

In interpersonal communication, our nonverbal body language says so much. Watching a marionette show in Salzburg, Austria, it struck me that the people manipulating the marionettes had to have a keen awareness of nonverbal body language in order to make their actions say the same thing that the script said. Actors on the stage must also be very conscious that their actions and facial expressions communicate effectively.

A letter communicates solely with words. A telephone call adds some nonverbal elements like voice tone, inflection, and volume. But face-to-face communication combines the words, the variations in voice, and the nonverbal language of body actions.

For Discussion/Reflection

When a close friend has an emotional story to tell, would you rather read it in a hand-written letter, read it in an e-mail message, hear it on the phone, or hear it in person? Why? Is a meeting by telephone conference as effective as an in-person meeting? What are the differences in meaning, understanding, and participation? What about a meeting by video conferencing?

---

* David W. Johnson in *Reaching Out: Interpersonal Effectiveness and Self-Actualization*, Sixth Edition (Boston: Allyn and Bacon, 1997), p. 172.

Nonverbal Communication

Most people are only subconsciously aware of nonverbal communication. We may get the message, but don't know exactly what gave us that message. By becoming more conscious of nonverbal aspects of communication, not only can we understand others better, but we can communicate our messages more effectively.

Nonverbal messages are transmitted through dress, posture, body tension, facial expression, degree of eye contact, hand and body movements, variations in speech, spatial distance, and touch. Since nonverbal messages are difficult to interpret accurately, conscious awareness of them is very important. The same nonverbal messages can mean very different things in different cultures, even in different parts of the same country. And the same nonverbal messages can mean quite different things in different situations. For example, crying can express happiness or sorrow, excitement or confusion. This is also a good reason not to take nonverbal cues too far. Folded arms can mean that a person is not receptive to what you are saying, but it can also indicate that the room is cold. Be careful!

The critical aspect of nonverbal communication is that it must agree with the verbal communication to be most effective. We only confuse the situation if our words say something different than our nonverbal messages. When verbal and nonverbal aspects of communication say the same thing, communication is more accurate and effective. Regardless of the ambiguity of nonverbal messages, conscious awareness of the nonverbal messages sent by others and sent by oneself can enhance understanding and make communication much more effective. By making conscious efforts to make nonverbal messages agree with verbal messages, you can strengthen the messages that you send.

For Discussion/Reflection

How is communication affected if the nonverbal message is different than the verbal message? Think of examples. Try acting out some extreme examples.

Exercise 1

Below is a list of feelings. Beside each feeling, write down ways to express the feeling nonverbally.

Feeling	Nonverbal Clues
Affection	Example: Touching, smiling, hugging, soft voice
Disgust	_____
Joy	_____
Sorrow	_____

Despair _____

Frustration _____

Interest _____

Indifference _____

Pain _____

Admiration _____

Shyness _____

Anger _____

Fear _____

Confidence _____

Exercise 2

Below is a very incomplete list of nonverbal cues. Beside each one, write down meanings that each could have.

Nonverbal Cue	Meaning
Touching	Example: Closeness, comfort, acceptance; intimidation, condescension
Frequent eye contact	_____
Arms folded	_____
Relaxed	_____
Calm voice	_____
Smile	_____
Fists clenched	_____
Shoulder shrug	_____

Squinted eyes   _____

Hand extended, open   _____

Jaws tightly closed   _____

Chin raised up   _____

Heavy sigh   _____

Wink   _____

Blank stare   _____

Exercise 3

Think of a compliment to give the person on your right. Go around the group, and have each person say the compliment to the person twice in a row. The first time, the person should use body language which shows that her or she is sincere. The second time, the person should use body language which shows that he or she does not mean it. The wording should be identical both times.

Exercise 4

Choose a feeling (from the list in Exercise 1) to act out without saying what the feeling is. As each person acts out the feeling nonverbally, the rest of the group should discuss which feeling the person is portraying.

As is true for many other communication skills, the development of effective nonverbal communication skills begins with a conscious awareness of them. Be aware of it in your everyday interaction with others. Strive to make your nonverbal cues say what your verbal messages say. The result will be a strengthened sense of effective communication.

For Next Time

Be particularly aware of nonverbal communication this week. Before the next meeting, do exercise 1 in Chapter 6 and read the section "Characteristics of the Responses."

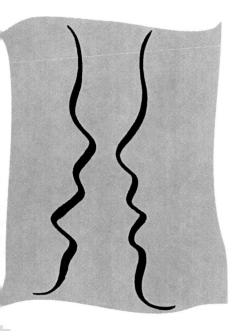

6
What Did You Say?
Active Listening

Effective listening is much more than just hearing what another person says. We have all found ourselves daydreaming during a lecture or sermon. We may have heard the words, but the meaning didn't register. This type of listening is not helpful when someone is talking about something of real concern to him or her. How can we listen and respond in ways that will help people solve problems, clarify feelings, or help build closer relationships?

Active listening involves both listening and responding. In listening and responding, the effectiveness of your help is greatly determined by your intentions and attitudes as you listen and give your response. The actual phrasing of your response is also important.

Exercise 1*

Instructions: In each of the following two situations, a person is describing a problem he or she is facing. After each scenario are five kinds of possible responses. Put a check mark by the response closest to the one you would use if someone approached you with that situation.

1. *Carlos:* I'm sick and tired of school. There is always studying that has to be done. Studying is for the birds. I don't know why I keep studying. I don't even know why I'm taking these classes. I don't have any idea what I want to do when I'm out of school. I think I'll just drop out and get a job somewhere at home.

   ___You're right, school is a pain. Maybe you should drop out and get a job at home. (E)

   ___You're getting tired of studying and are frustrated because you don't know what you want to do with your studies—is that it? (U)

---

* The exercises in this chapter are adapted from David W. Johnson, *Reaching Out: Interpersonal Effectiveness and Self-Actualization*, Sixth Edition (Boston: Allyn and Bacon, 1997), pp. 189-217. Adapted by permission.

___How much do you study? What classes are you taking? Is there a job at home that you could get? (P)

___Students often go through a stage where they're frustrated because they don't know where they're headed. You're just worried that you may have trouble finding a decent job after you graduate. (I)

___You have some good points. I see what you mean. I'm sure that whatever you decide will work out fine. (S)

2. *Carrie:* I'm disgusted with my roommates. They're so inconsiderate and always leave the place a mess. I always have to clean up after them because I'm embarrassed about the mess. They never do their share of the work.

___You're very picky about what the apartment looks like. You're too concerned about what other people think. You shouldn't get so upset. (I)

___I'm sure the girls will help more in the future. Give them time. When they see that you like the place neat, they'll be more considerate. (S)

___How long have you been living with them? Have they ever helped you clean the apartment? How much time do you spend keeping the place clean? (P)

___You're right. They shouldn't be so inconsiderate. You shouldn't have to always clean up after them. (E)

___You feel that you do an unfair amount of the work in the apartment. You think the other girls should help more, right? (U)

Notice that each of the responses in the exercise above has a letter after it. When someone wants to discuss a problem or concern of theirs with you, there are at least five ways in which you can listen and respond:

1. Advising and Evaluating (E)
2. Analyzing and Interpreting (I)
3. Reassuring and Supporting (S)
4. Questioning and Probing (P)
5. Paraphrasing and Understanding (U)

Spend a few minutes thinking about the way in which you respond. You probably use all of these responses at some time. Which of the five would you say you use the most? the least?

Characteristics of the Responses

Each response can be appropriate and effective, depending on the situation. Some, like the advising and evaluating response, must be used with great caution, and have the potential of straining relationships. Some are more helpful than others in building friendships and helping people explore further their feelings and thoughts. Each response reveals certain underlying intentions. Here are some characteristics of each type of response:

Advising and Evaluating (E)
- Gives advice and makes a judgment as to the relative goodness, appropriateness, effectiveness, and rightness of what the sender is thinking; communicates an evaluative, corrective, suggestive, or moralizing attitude or intent.
- Includes phrases such as, "If I were you, . . ." "One good way is . . ." "Why don't you . . .?" "You should . . ." "You ought to . . ." "The thing to do is . . ." and "Don't you think . . .?"
- Often builds barriers that keep you from being helpful and developing a deeper friendship.
- Can put others on the defensive, often closing their minds to new ideas.
- Often communicates that your judgment is superior. A person with a problem does not want to be made to feel inferior.
- Can be a way of avoiding involvement with another person's concerns and conflicts.
- Is quick and easy, but can communicate that you don't care enough to take the time to understand the problems fully.
- Advice can encourage people not to take responsibility for their own problems.
- Often tells more about your values, needs, and perspectives than about the other person's problems.

Other responses are usually, though not always, more helpful.

Analyzing and Interpreting (I)
- Shows the intention to teach, to tell the sender what his problem means, to inform him how he really feels about the situation, or to impart some psychological knowledge to the sender.
- Includes phrases such as, "Now I know what your problem is . . ." or "The reason you are upset is . . ."
- Often makes the sender defensive and will discourage him or her from revealing more thoughts and feelings.
- Communicates that, "I know more about you than you know about yourself." People generally resent this attitude.

Reassuring and Supporting (S)
- Indicates that you want to reassure, be sympathetic, or reduce the intensity of the sender's feelings.
- Includes phrases such as, "I'm sure everything will turn out all right," or "Things will be better tomorrow."
- Frequently communicates a lack of interest or understanding; it does nothing to clarify the causes and potential solutions for the depression.
- Often is a way of saying, "You should not feel as you do."

Questioning and Probing (P)
- Asks questions that indicate that you want to get further information, guide the discussion along certain lines, or bring the sender to a certain realization or conclusion that you have in mind.

Closed questions:
- Usually ask for a simple yes or no answer.
- Include questions like, "Do you like your job?"
- Usually less helpful than open questions.

Open questions:
- Encourage other people to answer at greater length and in more detail.
- Include questions like, "How do you feel about your job?"
- More helpful than closed questions because they encourage others to share more personal feelings and thoughts.
- Asking "Why?" questions puts people on the defensive because it encourages them to justify rather than explore their actions.
- "Why?" questions show disapproval or give advice. For example, "Why did you yell at the teacher?" implies "I don't think you should have yelled at the teacher."
- "What, where, when, how, and who" questions are generally more helpful; they allow people to be more specific, precise, and revealing.

Questions, while they can communicate that you are interested in helping, do not necessarily communicate that you understand. They may be more effective if changed to a reflective statement, discussed next.

Paraphrasing and Understanding (U)
- Indicates that your intent is to understand the sender's thoughts and feelings.
- Includes making reflective statements like, "You really like swimming," rather than asking, "Do you like swimming?"
- Can begin a clarifying and summarizing process that increases the accuracy of understanding.
- Often gives the sender a clearer understanding of him- or herself and of the implications of his or her present feelings and thinking.
- Reassures the sender that you are trying to understand his or her thoughts and feelings.
- Revolves around the notion that when a person expresses a message, and that message is paraphrased in fresh words with no change of its essential meaning, the person will expand upon or further explore the message so that it is more accurate and meaningful.
- Is the most effective way to communicate to a person that you are interested in him or her as a person and that you have an accurate understanding of what is being said; it most encourages further elaboration and exploration of the problem.
- May help you to see the problem from the other person's point of view.
- Showing a concern for what another person is saying and taking time to fully understand often makes the other person more willing to listen to what you have to say.
- Includes statements like, "So you felt really upset that . . .?" "You see yourself as . . ." and "Your understanding is that . . ."
- Helps open up communication.
- But can sound gimmicky if not done with sincerity and skill.

Many relationships or conversations are best begun using the understanding response until a trust level is established; then the other categories of response can be more reely used. Evaluative responses may be helpful when you are specifically asked to make a value judgment or when you wish to disclose your own values and attitudes. Probing responses will help get a clear definition of the problem if you don't understand what the person is talking about. Supportive responses are useful when the person needs to feel accepted or needs enough support to try to engage in behavior aimed at solving his or her problem. Interpretive responses are sometimes useful in confronting another person with the effect of the behavior on you; if carried out with skill, integrity, and empathy, it can be a powerful stimulus to growth.

For Discussion/Reflection

When you are telling a friend something that is extremely important to you, how would each of these five types of responses make you feel? What would encourage you to say more? What would cause you to stop talking or to be more guarded about what you say?

Exercise 2

Read the quotes below and write a response for each category.

1. *Christie:* I'm worried about my friend Cindy. She has a good job, but she's about to lose it because she often shows up to work late. She spends most of her money on nice clothes, and then she never has enough money for rent and food, so she borrows money from a lot of other people. I'm afraid that if she loses her job, she will really be in a lot of trouble.

   Evaluative Response:

   _____
   _____
   _____

   Interpretive Response:

   _____
   _____
   _____

   Supportive Response:

   _____
   _____
   _____

   Probing Response:

   _____
   _____
   _____

Understanding Response:

_____

_____

_____

2. *Kevin.*: I'm having a lot of trouble with my job. I usually get more work done than anyone else, but the boss always yells at me more than he yells at anyone else. He's really being unfair.

Evaluative Response:

_____

_____

_____

Interpretive Response:

_____

_____

_____

Supportive Response:

_____

_____

_____

Probing Response:

_____

_____

_____

Understanding Response:

_____

_____

_____

Developing the Paraphrasing or Understanding Response

Effective paraphrasing can be a very helpful tool. A paraphrasing response consists of several elements. The *content*, or actual wording of a response, is important. It is better to paraphrase the person's statement in your own words than to simply repeat what the person said. The *depth* of the response should match the depth of the person's statement. Don't respond lightly to a serious statement, or seriously to a shallow statement. It is important that your paraphrase does not add or abstract *meaning* from the person's message. Keep the language simple to ensure accurate communication.

Often paraphrasing responses can be more than statements. Starting the paraphrase with "As you view it . . .?" or "So, it seems to you . . .?" or ending the response with

"Is that it?" or "right?" turns the paraphrase into a question. This often increases the effectiveness of the paraphrasing response without making it a probing response.

For Discussion/Reflection

How often do people paraphrase when they are listening to someone else? Why do they use or avoid this listening response? Have you seen situations where paraphrasing was not helpful?

Exercise 3

Below are two quotes followed by four responses. Determine the appropriate classification from these choices and write the letter in the blank provided.

(I) Identical Content. Mostly repetition of the same words the person used.
(P) Paraphrasing Content. Rephrasing in fresh words without changing the meaning or tone of the person's statement.
(S) Shallow or Partial Meaning. A response which does not represent the person's full meaning.
(A) Additional Meaning. A response which adds meaning to what the person said.

1. "Dave sure makes me mad. He thinks and acts like he's so good at everything. He always makes other people feel so small. I just wish he would shut up for once!"

   ___You're a little bit upset with Dave, right?
   ___You hate Dave and never want to see him again.
   ___You're irritated with Dave because he is so arrogant and puts others down.
   ___Dave made you mad. He belittles others and you wish he would shut up.

2. "I'm tired of being at home. My parents argue a lot, and sometimes they take their frustration out on me. I sure wish they wouldn't get so upset."

   ___Your parents are planning a divorce, and you may run away, right?
   ___You're tired of being home because your parents argue a lot. You wish they wouldn't get so upset.
   ___It bothers you that your parents disagree and get so upset, is that it?
   ___Your parents don't always agree, right?

Pontius' Puddle

Learning the Skill of Paraphrasing

Paraphrasing is not the best response in all situations. (If someone runs up to you and asks you where the bathroom is, you shouldn't say, "Oh, you have to use the bathroom, right?") But paraphrasing can be effective in many discussions.

At first it is a challenge to make paraphrasing meaningful, to keep it from sounding gimmicky. Developing the skill of paraphrasing effectively is an important aspect of interpersonal communication. It is a form of active listening. Begin by making conscious efforts at paraphrasing, and the skill will become more and more natural.

Exercise 4

Write effective paraphrasing responses to each of the following statements:

1. "Stay out of my affairs. I've got enough problems without you getting your sticky fingers into the mess!"

   _____
   _____
   _____

2. "I have a report due in English tomorrow, dress rehearsal for tomorrow night's play, choir rehearsal tonight, and here you are, bugging me to work on your project! Why don't you just get off my back!"

   _____
   _____
   _____

3. "Every time I suggest something, you either ignore it or act like it's stupid!"

   _____
   _____
   _____

Developing any skill is a continuous process. Keep working at paraphrasing effectively. You will find that it is a very helpful skill in interpersonal communication.

For Discussion/Reflection

When people have a conflict, how soon do they usually identify the main issue? How does taking positions in a conflict interfere with the ability to address the underlying issues? How can underlying issues be addressed? How does paraphrasing help? In what other ways can underlying issues be addressed? What is the likely result if underlying issues are not determined and addressed?

For Next Time

Read through Chapter 7 before the next meeting.

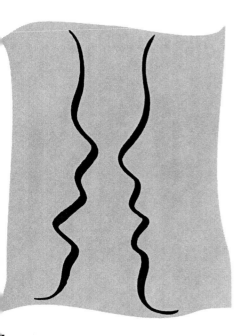

7
Speaking with Care

Listening skills and speaking skills go hand in hand. Paraphrasing could easily be called a speaking skill, but it is also a listening skill since effective paraphrasing requires careful listening. This session focuses more specifically on speaking skills, especially those that are useful in conflict situations.

Speaking for Yourself

It is important when communicating to own your statements. Using generalities to speak for others is unfair because it allows little possibility for accountability and further dialogue. Generalities about whose opinions you are expressing make it difficult to tell whether you really think and feel what you are saying or whether you are simply repeating the thoughts of others. Examples of *not* speaking for yourself:

"Most people here don't want to . . ."

"Some of our friends . . ."

"Anyone can see just by looking that . . ."

"Everyone knows that . . ."

"I'm only speaking for those who have talked with me but are afraid to speak out . . ."

Only you are an expert on your ideas, beliefs, feelings, and needs. Only *others* are experts on their ideas, beliefs, feelings, and needs. Speaking for others with generalities can do nothing but create ambiguity. Speaking for yourself means taking responsibility for your comments. It means being honest and, in fact, being assertive since you, and no one else, are accountable for your comments. It adds clarity to communication and opens the door to further and more beneficial discussion. Examples of speaking for yourself:

"I feel that. . ."

"I want to . . ."

"My impression is that . . ."

"In my opinion . . ."

"I disagree that. . ."

Be Specific

If you can't be specific, or speak in concrete examples, you are likely not in a position to communicate helpfully to others. Specificity enhances communication. Generalities almost always contribute to misunderstandings: Examples of *not* being specific:

"The problem here is jealousy . . ."

"People around here are cold and unfriendly . . ."

"You have a very poor attitude . . ."

"You're irresponsible . . ."

"You're always offending people . . ."

". . . and other things like that."

Being specific means:
- Speaking in a way that others can *do* something about what you are saying.
- Concentrating on *saying* what you *mean*.
- Speaking in terms of WHO is doing (or not doing) WHAT to WHOM, WHEN, and WHERE. Be able to speak to at least three of these.
- Speaking in terms of people's *actions,* not about who they are or what their personal traits or motivations are. This decreases the defensive feelings people have as a result of your statements.
- Not exaggerating. Don't use absolute words in less-than-absolute situations. Absolute terms like *always, everyone, no one, every,* and *never* are not helpful in communication when the terms are not accurate. Most people would have a hard time believing a statement like, "You are *never* on time!" There is little reason to believe that your other statements are any more accurate than this one if you make exaggerated statements like that.
- A commitment to loving, caring, and being honest by openly focusing comments on action, rather than attacking negative personality traits.

Using statements like:
- "I feel as though others don't like me when I come to church and go home again without anyone talking with me."
- "In the last month I felt as though you were criticizing me publicly on three separate occasions, and I'm beginning to feel as though you don't respect my judgment. Could we sit down and try to talk things through tomorrow?"
- "When you suggested a minute ago that I didn't care about the unity of this team, it made me feel angry and misunderstood."

The Specific I Message

A "Specific I Message" contains three components when confronting objectionable behavior:

1. It states the feelings or needs of the speaker.
2. It states specifically the objectionable behavior of the other person.
3. It identifies the consequences of the objectionable behavior to the speaker.

Speaking for Yourself + Being Specific = the "Specific I Message"

Some examples:

- "I get irritated when you arrive late for our study session because it upsets my schedule for the rest of the morning."
- "I really felt angry this morning when you criticized me with three other people nearby. It made me feel as though you were intentionally trying to humiliate me in public."
- "I'm feeling pretty upset and hurt, and I'd like to discuss things with you a bit. On several occasions recently I've asked you if there is anything you would like to change in the way our committee operates. You always said no. Then yesterday, without any warning, you reported to the pastor that we were having difficulties. I'm angry because it makes me feel as though you weren't really leveling with me or taking me seriously."
- "I was hurt last night when you yelled at me in front of my friends. I've asked you before whether it bothered you if we listened to your records, and you always said it didn't. I'm angry because you embarrassed me in front of my friends when I had your permission for what I was doing."

Putting "I" in front of a statement does *not* automatically make it a Specific I Message. "I don't like it that you're so irresponsible" is no more a Specific I Message than "You're so irresponsible." Specific I Messages take more than that!

Think of a situation where it would have been helpful for you to use the Specific I Message. Think of an appropriate message for that situation and write it here. Be sure to be specific and to speak for yourself.

1. A married couple was driving on an icy road one night. The woman was uncomfortable because the road was icy, and told her husband, "You're driving too fast." He had been raised on a farm, and felt he was a good, experienced driver. He was insulted that she didn't think he could handle the situation. In reaction to what she had said, he actually sped up, making her even more uncomfortable.

   The next day the couple talked about the incident. They decided that they had not handled the situation well. She did not really say what she meant, and threatened him by saying "You . . ." If she had said what she meant, "I'm nervous because the road is icy," he likely would have slowed down, and she would have been more comfortable.

2. When I was a little boy, I came into the house on a cold winter day, and as I often did, left the door open. Instead of getting disgusted and yelling for me to shut the door, my Mother said, "The door is open, and I'm cold." She heard me mumbling, "I'd better shut the door." I did. And no one got upset. The Specific I Message did the trick.

For Discussion/Reflection

Have you seen Specific I Messages used in a way that kept communication open? What is the key? Do people often use Specific I Messages when they communicate about something that upsets them? Why or why not?

Exercise 1

Write an example of a Specific I Message which would more effectively replace the following statements.

1. You're very inconsiderate. Why don't you ever help clean up this place?

_____

_____

2. You're just a big gossip! Why don't you ever keep what I tell you to yourself?

_____

_____

Five Skills for Effective Communication

1. Be careful about evaluating and interpreting.
While there is sometimes a place for evaluation and interpretation in active listening (see Chapter 6), it becomes dangerous when speaking in a situation of conflict. In such circumstances, describe other people's behavior without evaluating or interpreting. To do so amounts to an aggressive response, which is an attack on the person. Avoid saying things like, "You're a rotten, self-centered egotist who won't listen to anyone else's ideas." Rather, say something like, "It bothers me that you keep interrupting me."

2. Don't talk behind someone else's back.
Talking about others in a situation where they don't have the opportunity to respond and benefit from your comments is not a useful form of communication. Unfortunately, though, it is common. It is easier than face-to-face confrontation, but the results are often negative. If you have a complaint, the best way to have something done about it and to maintain integrity is to deal head-on with your complaint.

When someone criticizes another to you without that person present, rather than pass the information on or set yourself up for a situation where you may be forced to speak for another ("I'm only speaking for those who've talked with me but are afraid to speak out . . ."), suggest that he or she talks directly to the person being criticized. In other words, encourage others to speak for themselves rather than have others speak for them. This is a much more effective form of communication. Perhaps you could offer to help formulate his or her thoughts in advance or even offer to be present as a mediator.

3. Ask for feedback.
To know how the receiver is interpreting your messages, ask for feedback as to what meanings the receiver is attaching to your messages. These phrases would often produce helpful feedback:
> "Do you see what I mean?"
> "Does that make sense to you?"
> "How does that sound?"
> "Are you with me?"

f it is critical that what you said is understood, it may even be appropriate at times to ask the person to paraphrase what you said.

4. Recognize that others' views are valid.

In conflicts, two parties disagree, but each party feels he or she is right. While you may quite strongly disagree with the other person, it can be helpful to show that you understand why he or she feels as he or she does. The message that, "I disagree with what you're saying, but I can understand why you feel that way," does not compromise your opinion, and yet it shows that you respect the other person. This can be very helpful in approaching a resolution to a disagreement. You may be right, but the other person's views are still valid.

5. Suggest "yesable propositions."

Another way to encourage positive results from Specific I Message confrontations is to use what Roger Fisher refers to in international politics as "Yesable Propositions."* These are questions which require a yes or no answer. The important thing to remember when suggesting an idea is to make it something which the other person not only *could* do, but which it could reasonably be expected that the other person *would* do.

To resolve a conflict situation, propose a solution such as the following: "Could we work out a schedule so that I'll clean this week, and then we'll alternate, with each of us cleaning every other week?" or "If I am sure to tell you if I want something kept confidential, would you agree not to mention it to anyone else?"

For Discussion/Reflection

In what ways do these skills make for effective communication? What other skills or principles would you add to the list? What would your list of things to avoid for effective communication include?

Positions and Interests

Consider the difference between positions and interests. People in conflict often think and talk in terms of their *positions*, which are statements or demands phrased as solutions. They are often "loaded" statements, reflecting unspoken information and hidden agenda. They reflect but do not state the interests of the person. *Interests* state the needs, concerns, and hopes of the person.

Talking in terms of positions instead of interests could be deliberate, but it more likely is unintentional. Without meaning to, people get locked into thinking of their proposed solution (position) without reflecting deliberately on their interests; or they may have thought about their interests and defined them in terms of positions because they don't see any alternatives. They often find the emotion that revolves around their interests gets in the way of defining them clearly.

In conflict, if the issue is defined in terms of positions, then creative, win/win problem solving is unlikely. People working from two differing positions may never discover the

---

* from Roger Fisher, *International Conflict for Beginners* (New York: Harper and Row, 1969), pp. 15-26.

underlying interests and, thus, may never be able to reach a collaborative solution. (You may want to look back to Chapter 1, and its survey of approaches to conflict.) However, if the issue is defined in terms of interests, the people are already much closer to finding a win-win solution.

Exercise 2
Positions versus Interests

After reviewing the initial two examples in the chart, try to change the remaining Position statements into Interest statements, and the remaining Interest statements into Position statements. Be creative. In all of the situations, how does the Interest statement help suggest new possibilities or solutions that are not evident from the Position statement?

Position Statement	Interest Statement	New Possibilities Suggested by the Interest Statement
Example 1: Maria says to her housemates: "I must have a room to myself."	"I am going to be working at night, so I need a quiet place to sleep during the day."	Sarah will also be working at night and could share a room with Maria.
Example 2: David says "I must have the car tonight."	"I have an important meeting at school at 7:00 this evening, and I am leading the meeting so I can't be late."	Greg is going to school for play practice at 6:30 and could take David.
I have to have a new computer.	(group fills in)	(group fills in)
You must replace the lawnmower you ruined.	(group fills in)	(group fills in)
(group fills in)	It is important that we start the meeting on time tonight because I have another meeting after this meeting.	(group fills in)
(group fills in)	After you drove my car, the tire was ruined because it had been driven flat too long. A new tire cost $80. The old tire had about half of its tread, so could you pay for half of the new tire?	(group fills in)

Interests Help, But Don't Solve Everything

Stating interests rather than positions helps work toward and reach collaborative solutions because it focuses the discussion on the real issues. It is not, however, a guarantee that a collaborative solution will be obvious. For example, in Example 1 above, if

Maria is not going to be working at night, that new possibility is not necessarily available. But by focusing on Maria's reason for wanting her own room, other ways to address her needs may be found. Don't give up if new possibilities or a solution are not obvious or easy. Collaborative problem-solving takes work!

For Discussion/Reflection

Review letters to the editor on particularly sensitive issues in local newspapers, or in church periodicals. What types of communication skills do the letters reflect? What view of conflict and conflict management do they reflect?

For Next Time

Read Chapter 8, up to Exercise 1.

8
What If the Other Person Is a Complete Idiot?

Toward the end of a workshop on communicating in conflict situations, there was time for questions. "What do you do if the guy's a complete idiot?" a man asked. Aside from the initial laughter, this was a very good question. Ideally, everyone would be skilled in conflict resolution, and it would be a simple process. In reality, not everyone is, and some people are quite obnoxious in conflict. What do you do then?

First of all, we must be careful to avoid an attitude toward conflict resolution which has hidden assumptions like these tacked on in parentheses:

You're entitled to your opinion (as long as it doesn't take you too long to change it and realize that I'm right).

I'd like to find a solution we can both live with (as long as it is identical to my position).

I'm willing to bend a little if you are (as long as you bend a lot more than I will).

We need to resolve this conflict (as long as you realize the conflict was your fault in the first place).

This kind of approach can lead to the attitude that the *other* person is not being fair (because he or she doesn't agree with my unreasonable ideas). We need to be careful that we don't get drawn into this kind of thinking. We need to see things from the other's point of view, and we need to acknowledge that we, too, may be partly at fault.

The Bible teaches us to have compassion, empathy, and understanding for others; to bend over backward, even, for our enemies. And we are told not to judge others (Matt. 7:1,2). As we have seen, the Bible does not address whether to resolve conflict, but *how* to. Conflict resolution is not simple, but the rewards are great. We must work hard to resolve conflict, and if the other person is not skilled in the resolving conflict, we must be willing to contribute even more than the situation actually warrants.

The concepts of assertiveness, honesty, and Specific I Messages are of particular relevance here. If someone is simply not being fair in a conflict situation, say so! It is much more productive to say, "I feel that we need to resolve this conflict because it will be better for both of us. I feel that you are not being fair by . . ." than to resort to the same unfair tactics the other person is using.

There is a specific format which is useful in almost any interpersonal dispute. The structure can be applied formally to more intense disputes. If you see that you're not making any progress in resolving a conflict, try this format. If the other person *is* being unfair, the confines of this structure may make the situation more manageable.

A Procedure for Discussing Interpersonal Conflict*

1. List the things you need to talk about.

2. Agree on ground rules.

   a. Each side will listen without interrupting while the other side presents its case. (Be brief.)
   b. Each side will summarize the other's case to the satisfaction of the other before discussing the issues.

3. Person A states his or her case while Person B listens. When A is finished, B summarizes A's case in his or her own words. (B must keep trying until A is satisfied that B is stating things accurately from A's perspective.)

4. B states his or her own case, and A summarizes.

5. List any areas of agreement that may have appeared (often quite a few).

6. List areas where you disagree and state precisely *how* you disagree. (Example: "A feels that . . . B differs in that . . .")

7. Discuss possible solutions.

8. State any solutions you work out in precise form. *Who* will do (or not do) *what*, *when*, and *where*? Writing it out helps to get it clear and precise.

9. Does the procedure need professional mediation? How could that be set up? (Refer ahead to Chapter 9.)

Step 5 is very helpful. Recognizing areas of agreement can make working with differences much easier. They can even be things like agreeing that you need to solve the problem.

In discussing possible solutions, brainstorming with no effort to be highly practical can be very effective. List the ideas quickly without discussing their merits. Then go back

---

* This procedure was presented as a worksheet by Ron Kraybill in the "Peacemaking and Conflict Resolution" class at Bethel College, North Newton, Kan., in the spring of 1982.

and work through the ideas, one by one. Even if all of the ideas are impractical, they may give you other ideas which might be useful.

Solutions can be quite involved (as in dealing with a wrecked car that was borrowed), or they can be a simple apology. Aim to find a solution that benefits *both* parties. Solutions need to reflect a *win/win* approach to conflict rather than a *win/lose* approach. Make solutions balanced, specific, realistic, clear, and simple.

The procedure for discussing interpersonal conflict can be a helpful way to structure discussion even when there are no hard feelings involved. Even without the formal structure, and even if the other person is unaware of these skills, knowledge of the procedure is helpful. Use the structure by just having one person informally try to follow it in this situation.

For Discussion/Reflection

What is the purpose for each step in the procedure? Have you seen this procedure used, either informally or formally? What were the results? Think of someone who does a good job of dealing with conflict. What makes that person effective?

Example of dialogue using the "Procedure for Discussing Interpersonal Conflict"

Todd and Roger have purchased a car together. They agreed to split the cost of the car exactly in half. Also, each will pay half of all expenses, such as insurance, maintenance, and repair costs. The cost of gas will be determined by the number of miles each drives the car. Todd drives the car more than Roger. When Todd was driving the car, it broke down. The repair bill is $200. Todd is speaking calmly throughout, but Roger is very loud and upset at first.

Todd: Roger, the repair bill for our car is $200. How soon can you get me your half?

Roger: My half? What are you talking about? You were driving the car. I'm not going to help pay.

Todd: But we agreed to split the costs of all repairs.

Roger: No we didn't! We split the cost of the car and maintenance. But I'm not responsible if something goes wrong when you're driving the car. I can't afford that. I suppose you're going to want to split the cost of the clothes you bought today, too. Forget it!

Todd: You know as well as I do that the breakdown wasn't my fault.

Roger: No, I don't! Then why does something always go wrong when *you're* driving, and I've never had any trouble? You must be a terrible driver.

Todd: I'm sorry that you feel that way. I think it would benefit us both if we would work through this conflict. I know of a procedure designed to resolve conflicts. Would you be willing to try and work through it? It will help us both understand each other's position better.

Roger: My mind's made up. As long as this stupid thing makes you see that, it's fine with me.

(Todd explains the procedure to Roger.)

Todd: It's pretty clear that we need to talk about who will pay the repair bills for the car. Is there anything else?

Roger: No, that's about it.

(Todd and Roger agree to the ground rules.)

Todd: OK. Why don't you start. What is your view about the repair bills for the car?

Roger: I thought you knew! I don't think that I should have to pay for repair bills for the car. I hardly ever drive the car, and it always breaks down while you're driving, so you should have to pay the bill.

Todd: What you're saying is that you feel that since you don't drive the car much, you shouldn't have to pay any of the repair bill, and you feel that since I was driving when the car broke down, I should have to pay. Is that right?

Roger: Yeah, pretty close.

Todd: OK. I agree that I drive the car more than you do, but you do drive the car some.

Roger: Yeah, but not near as much as you do.

Todd: Remember, we agreed not to interrupt each other. If you disagree with what I say, you can tell me later. I drive the car more, but you do drive it some. Most times when the car breaks down, it is just due to normal wear and tear, and is not the driver's fault. I don't feel that this problem was my fault. It is just the result of using the car, so I feel you should help pay for it. Can you summarize what I said?

Roger: You said the same thing you've always been saying, that you want me to pay half of the repair bill.

Todd: I don't feel you understand all that I said.

Roger: OK. You said you drive more, but the breakdown wasn't your fault, and you want me to help pay. Right?

Todd: OK. Well, we agree on several things. First, we both agree that the car broke down and that the repair bill needs to be paid.

Roger: Yeah, and we both agree that you drive the car a lot more than I do.

Todd: Anything else?

Roger: No, that's it, I think.

Todd: So where do we disagree?

Roger: You think I should pay half of the bill, and I don't. That's about it.

Todd: And you think that the breakdown was my fault because I was driving.

Roger: Well, my main point was that I use the car less and so you are putting on more miles and causing more of the breakdowns. So how can we resolve the problem? Well, you could pay the bill, or we could sell the car. Hey, you could buy my half of the car from me!

Todd: I can't afford that, and you do use the car some. When we buy gas, we split the cost according to how many miles we've driven. How would it work if we did the same for car repairs?

Roger: That sounds OK. That means I won't have to pay much.

Todd: Right. That sounds fair to me, since I use it more. You will have to pay some, though.

Roger: OK, but it will be a lot less than half.

Todd: How should we figure out who pays how much?

Roger: Let's decide who drove what percentage of the last 500 miles, and divide the bill by those percentages.

Todd: OK. I'll write that down and put it in the glove box. We both agree, then, to pay the percentage of the repair bill according to the percentage we each drive the car. Can you agree to give me your share as soon as we get the repair bill, and then I'll be in charge of paying them?

Roger: Yeah, that sounds fine.

Exercise 1
Applying the "Procedure for Discussing Interpersonal Conflict"

It is not necessary to apply the procedure rigidly to all interpersonal conflicts, but in the following exercise you are nevertheless encouraged to use all the steps as a way of working at the skills.

For each conflict situation described below, divide into groups of three. One will be person "A," another person "B," and the third will be an observer. Each person reads the appropriate information. A should not read B's material, and B should not read A's. Then persons A and B work through the conflict using the procedure described earlier. Person A is very angry and should exaggerate the anger. Person B is trying to use the skills developed in these sessions (assertiveness, the Specific I Message, paraphrasing, speaking skills, etc.). The third person observes and afterward evaluates person B's performance, using these guidelines:

Was B assertive, but not aggressive?
Did B paraphrase effectively?
Did B speak for him- or herself?
Was B honest?
Was B specific?
Did B use the Specific I Message?
Did B stay away from evaluating and interpreting?
Did B avoid exaggerating?
Did B recognize that A's views were valid?
Did B propose a Yesable Proposition?
Did B focus on Positions or Interests?

Situation 1

A and B are chemistry lab partners and must share lab equipment. However, they must do separate work.

Person A

B has been using more than her share of equipment, putting it away dirty, copying your results, and just being a big pain. Your lab grade is suffering. You are mad that she is so inconsiderate and cheats. Finally, you've just had too much. You plan to set her straight.

Person B

You have been working hard to get a good lab grade. You always ask before you use the equipment. You occasionally compare your results with your partner's to make sure you are doing things right.

Situation 2

Person A

You have an old lawn mower which has been causing you a little trouble, but which would still be good for quite a while. A new one would cost about $350. Person B borrowed it and returned it broken. The mechanic says it is not worth fixing. You feel that Person B took very poor care of it while using it. You expect him to buy you a new one.

Person B

You borrowed A's lawn mower. You accidentally ran over something and the lawn mower quit on you. It was real old and almost shot anyway. A new one like it would cost about $300. You could feel good about paying a little to help replace it, but since it was almost ruined already, you don't think you should pay much.

Situation 3

B wishes to sell his car, and advertises it in the newspaper. A sees the advertisement and goes to look a. the car. A and B know each other only a very little. A decides to buy the car for $2,000. One week after A buys the car, the engine locks up and is ruined. A goes to B to discuss the situation.

Person A

You know enough about cars to know that if the car had been cared for properly, the engine would not lock up like that. Person B led you to believe that the car was in great shape and had been cared for very carefully. Person B obviously lied to you and was covering up. He'd better give you your money back.

Person B

You are not mechanically minded, but you are sure that you were never extremely careless with the car's upkeep. Sure, you may have worked the car hard sometimes, and maintenance may not always have been done on schedule, but there was no blatant misuse of the car. There was no way that you could know that the engine would be ruined soon—that was the chance that person B had to take.

The skills which this exercise should help develop are at the heart of interpersonal communication, and this procedure can be helpful in a variety of actual conflict situations. Keep this in mind as you deal with conflict, even if others know nothing of it. If appropriate, explain the procedure to the other person and try to formally follow the procedure.

For Discussion/Reflection

When people have a conflict, how often do they identify the main issue immediately? How does taking positions in a conflict interfere with the ability to address the underlying issues? How can underlying issues be addressed? How do Specific I Messages and Paraphrasing help? How does the Procedure for Discussing Interpersonal Conflict help address underlying issues? In what other ways can underlying issues be addressed? What is the likely result if underlying issues are not determined and addressed?

Look back at the discussion of Positions versus Interests in Chapter 7. How can the procedure for discussing interpersonal conflict in this session help identify and focus the interests and positions?

For Next Time

Read Chapter 9 before the next meeting.

Prayer of St. Francis

Make me a channel of Your peace.
Where there is hatred, let me bring Your love.
Where there is injury, Your pardon, Lord.
And where there's doubt, true faith in You.

Make me a channel of Your peace.
Where there's despair in life, let me bring hope.
Where there is darkness, only light,
And where there's sadness ever joy.

Oh Master, grant that I may never seek
So much to be consoled as to console,
To be understood as to understand,
To be loved, as to love, with all my soul.

Make me a channel of Your peace.
It is in pardoning that we are pardoned,
In giving to all [men] that we receive,
And in dying that we're born to eternal life.

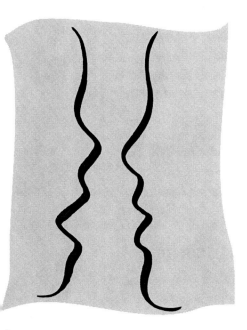

9

The Third Party and Conflict

It can be very frustrating and can hurt deeply when you see other people getting nowhere in a disagreement, allowing the conflict to build a barrier between them. The burden is especially heavy when we consider that the Bible gives the church the authority and obligation to settle disagreements.

Review again Matthew 18:15-20; Philippians 4:2-3; and Matthew 5:23-24. Then look back at the "Procedure for Discussing Interpersonal Conflict" in Session 8 (page XX). This basic procedure is also helpful as a mediation procedure where a third party helps guide two people with a conflict through the procedure. Have you seen this procedure (or something like it in use? What were the results? How can a third party help guide the procedure?

Exercise 1

This exercise is intended to help you grapple with the benefits and the difficulties of third-party intervention in conflict. Divide into smaller groups of four. Use the situations in Chapter 8 or create your own situations for some third-party role playing. Have two people be the parties in conflict, one a mediator to help guide the process, using the procedure outlined on page 53, and one an observer. Go through the role plays, even if it feels artificial to you.

Following the exercise discuss together: What advantages were there in having a third party involved in the conflict. How credible was the third party? What made the third person effective in dealing with the conflict?

Helping Others Resolve a Conflict

The "Procedure for Discussing Interpersonal Conflict" (page 53) is especially useful in a case where a third person intervenes. The third person can serve as mediator, someone who keeps the others accountable to the steps of the procedure. As the third person, you would not be in a position to *decide* the outcome of the conflict. Rather, your role would be to help the two people who disagree find a mutually acceptable solution.

As a go-between, you have the unique opportunity to remain neutral. Your neutrality will enhance the environment for resolving the conflict. If one of the conflicting persons is not being fair or is not showing that he or she is committed to resolving the conflict, you can point out that both persons stand to gain from the resolution of the conflict. Stress the win/win nature of the resolution; no one needs to lose.

As a third party, you can put to work all the skills used so far in this study. But you are also in a position to encourage others in using the skills. You can ask them to paraphrase, for example, or to hold them to Specific I Messages. You can use the conflict to pass on your own learnings. However . . .

Caution! Third-party Involvement Needs Much Discernment

This study has focused primarily on communication skills that help us deal with our own interpersonal conflict, or that of people who are close to us. Helping others resolve conflict can be a difficult and delicate task, and one that should not be taken lightly, or entered into blindly. Some seem naturally gifted to help others work through their disagreements. Others are not as gifted. Often, conflicts in neighborhoods and churches are best dealt with through the assistance of professional mediators or people who have received special training.

The remainder of this chapter explores the main forms of conflict resolution facilitated by third parties. By looking at them side by side, we can see the main differences between them, as well as the advantages and disadvantages of each. From this survey, you may wish to pursue further experience or studies. You may also find ways to combine the interpersonal skills you have developed in the previous sessions with ideas generated here, to help you as you respond to, and help deal with, conflict you may encounter.

Four Forms of Conflict Resolution

There are four basic ways in which people attempt to resolve conflict: negotiation, mediation, arbitration, and litigation. Third-party intervention is integral to the latter three, and is often used in the first.

NEGOTIATION is largely what this study has equipped you to do at an interpersonal level, and most often happens without third-party intervention. Negotiation can, however, involve third parties who represent the two sides in a conflict.

MEDIATION: A third party (mediator) helps the parties talk with each other, and helps with the process of resolving their differences.

ARBITRATION: A third party, the arbitrator, hears arguments of the parties (or their lawyers) and presents a decision to resolve the conflict. The decision could be advisory (not binding) or binding, depending on the circumstances.

LITIGATION: A third party (judge or jury) hears arguments of the parties or their lawyers, and issues a binding decision.

There are many variations of these basic forms. Negotiation can be informal, or can involve representatives who negotiate for the parties. Mediation principles can be part of a very informal process (conciliation or facilitation), or can be a formal, structured process; it can be ordered by a court of law, or can even be conducted by a judge as a settlement conference. Another variation is a process called Med-Arb in which, as the name suggests, a third party tries to mediate the conflict, but, if mediation is unsuccessful, arbitrates and presents a decision.

Issues That Determine the Effectiveness of Third-Party Intervention

The following are questions that must be addressed when parties in a conflict call in outside help. Consider the questions in light of what you have learned so far in this study:

Entry into conflict. How does a third person become involved in a conflict? Is the process of selection fair? How is trust developed, and how is trust destroyed?

Role of the third party. What could a third person's role be in helping two people work through the conflict—for example, in using the Procedure for Discussing Interpersonal Conflict (page 53)? How can a third party help "uncover" Interests so the parties are not dealing only with Positions? (You may want to look back at Chapter 7 where those terms are discussed.) What is the difference between the Process and the Outcome? What is the third person's role with respect to the Process? With respect to the Outcome?

Neutrality of the third party. Often, the third person's role is described as being neutral. How can a person who is neutral help in a way that someone who isn't neutral cannot? What should a neutral third person do if she sees something extremely unfair or unjust in the way the parties are resolving a conflict? What if the third person learns something confidential about the other person? Can she still remain neutral? What if one person is very powerful or articulate, and the other is not? What is the third person's role in that situation?

Cultural Differences. How do cultural differences affect the role of the third party? Would the role of third party be different in different cultures? What happens when the conflict is between people from different cultural backgrounds?

Exercise 2

Diagram how each of the four main procedures (Negotiation, Mediation, Arbitration, and Litigation) would look by drawing X's and O's (or more letters, if needed) representing the main people involved, along with an aerial view of whatever tables and chairs are needed. How many people are involved? How many tables are there? Who sits where? Use arrows to show where the communication takes place. What significance do each of these questions have for how the process works? For example, direct negotiation (without representatives) may look like this:

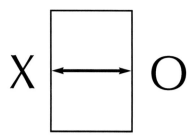

Diagram what Mediation, Arbitration, and Litigation would look like.

Exercise 3

Divide into groups to role-play each of the four main procedures, or, if you have time, create scripts for skits that may be performed in your group. Use one of the situations described in Chapter 8, or one or two of the following:

- Two people who have lived together for several years want to arrange terms by which one of them moves out.
- Two people who are building a house disagree over the floor plan. They need a solution.
- Two neighbors in an apartment building are trying to settle a dispute over loud music and parties.
- A landlord and a tenant disagree about what maintenance priorities and property improvements are essential.
- A husband and wife, who have very different tastes in entertainment, nevertheless want to be together when they go out. They are trying to plan when and where to go.
- Two farmers try to come to a settlement over a serious mistake. One of them sprayed his field by airplane, and by mistake sprayed his neighbor's field and ruined the crop.

Again, consider the questions posed in the previous exercise on Diagramming, and these additional questions: Where are the people looking? Who does the talking? What is each person wearing (jeans, suit and tie, robe)? What happens when the process is completed? Again, what significance do each of these questions have for how the process works?

For Discussion/Reflection

Think of a conflict you have been involved in, or have witnessed, in which the disagreements just escalated and grew into something no one anticipated or expected. Could a skilled third person have helped the situation? Could an ineffective third person have made things worse? How?

Exercise 4

Compare the four conflict resolution procedures by filling out the chart below.*

	Negotiation	Mediation	Arbitration	Litigation
Who is involved?				
Is there a neutral person?				
What is the role of the neutral?				
What is the role of the parties with the conflict?				
What role do the disputing parties have?				
What type of proceeding is it? (private, public, confidential, formal, flexible)				
Who controls the proceeding?				
What rules apply?				
How will positions and interests be stated?				
Whose role is it to "uncover" interests?				
How formal is the procedure?				
Who makes the final decision?				
When might the procedure be appropriate?				
How much does it cost (financially, emotionally)?				
What are the advantages?				
What are the disadvantages?				

* This exercise is based on the Alternate Dispute Resolution chart of the *Manual on Alternate Dispute Resolution*, from the ADR Committee of the Colorado Bar Association, 1992.

For Discussion/Reflection

Consider the following Biblical examples where third persons were involved in conflict resolution: I Kings 3:16-28; Matthew 22:15-22; John 4:5-26; John 8:1-11; Acts 15:36-41; Philippians 4:2, 3. See also Matthew 5:23-26; Matthew 18:15-20; I Corinthians 6:1-6; Galatians 6:1. What models of third person intervention are given? In what ways do they inform the conflict transformation work you observe in your life?

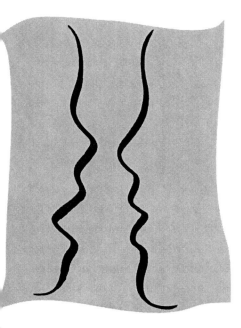

10
Made in God's Image

Then God said, "Let us make humankind in our image, according to our likeness; and let them have dominion over the fish of the sea, and over the birds of the air, and over the cattle, and over all the wild animals of the earth, and over every creeping thing that creeps upon the earth." So God created humankind in his image, in the image of God he created them; male and female he created them. God blessed them, and God said to them, "Be fruitful and multiply, and fill the earth and subdue it, and have dominion over the fish of the sea and over the birds of the air and over every living thing that moves upon the earth.

God said, "See, I have given you every plant yielding seed that is upon the face of all the earth, and every tree with seed in its fruit; you shall have them for food. And to every beast of the earth, and to every bird of the air, and to everything that creeps on the earth, everything that has the breath of life, I have given every green plant for food." And it was so. God saw everything that he had made, and indeed, it was very good. And there was evening and there was morning, the sixth day. (Genesis 1:26-31)

What kind of image do you have of yourself? What kind of self-image do you convey to others? If you were to describe yourself, would you use positive adjectives like those listed on page 66, or would you use more negative ones?

Every one of us is created in God's image. What does that mean for you? You may be wary of being boastful, arrogant, or too proud. But that doesn't mean you shouldn't feel good about who you are, and the unique gifts you possess.

If you feel good about yourself, it is easier to show others that you accept them, too. Compliments are a very powerful binding force. They feel good. They give the receiver a warm feeling of acceptance toward the one giving the compliment. A good way to grow in communication skills, therefore is to learn to accept compliments, and be more open in giving them. This is one way that you can show God's love.

Compliments are also effective in reducing any feelings of hostility toward people with whom we are in conflict; it is difficult to be angry with someone who is sincere in giving you a compliment. Compliments very effectively build others up and open lines of communication.

For Discussion/Reflection

What kind of a self-image do you convey to others? What does being created in the image of God mean to you? What are your most significant skills and gifts in areas related to conflict resolution? What areas could you develop further? Do you feel comfortable complimenting or encouraging others? Why or why not? Who would you encourage to pursue their skills in helping others resolve conflicts?

Exercise 1

Write your name at the top of the list of adjectives. Hand your book to the person on the right. Keep rotating the books to the right until everyone has had everyone else's book. Everyone should check (✘) three adjectives that describe the person whose name is at the top. Add positive adjectives to the list if you think of some that would be appropriate. Check adjectives that have already been checked, if you wish, but each person should check off at least one (but no more than three) adjective that has not already been checked.

Your name: _____

able ____	empathetic ____	kind ____	quiet ____	simple ____
accepting ____	energetic ____	knowledgeable____	radical ____	sincere ____
adaptable ____	even-tempered ____	learned ____	rational ____	skillful ____
admirable ____	fair ____	lively ____	realistic ____	sociable ____
ambitious ____	forgiving ____	logical ____	reasonable ____	specific ____
assertive ____	frank ____	loving ____	reassuring ____	spontaneous ____
authoritative ____	free ____	mature ____	receptive ____	stable ____
bold ____	friendly ____	merry ____	reflective ____	strong ____
brave ____	generous ____	moderate ____	relaxed ____	sympathetic ____
calm ____	genial ____	modest ____	reliable ____	tactful ____
carefree ____	gentle ____	normal ____	religious ____	tender ____
caring ____	giving ____	observant ____	reserved ____	thoughtful ____
charming ____	good-natured ____	open-minded ____	respectable ____	tolerant ____
cheerful ____	happy ____	optimistic ____	respectful ____	trusting ____
clever ____	harmonious ____	organized ____	responsible ____	trustworthy ____
confident ____	helpful ____	original ____	responsive ____	understanding ____
collaborative ____	high-spirited ____	outspoken ____	satisfied ____	useful ____
considerate ____	honest ____	passive ____	scientific ____	visionary ____
controlled ____	honorable ____	patient ____	searching ____	warm ____
cordial ____	humble ____	peaceful ____	self-accepting ____	well-disciplined____
courageous ____	idealistic ____	perceptive ____	self-assertive ____	willful ____
dependable ____	imaginative ____	perfectionist ____	self-aware ____	wise ____
determined ____	innovative ____	persuasive ____	self-conscious ____	worthy ____
devout ____	inspiring ____	playful ____	self-reliant ____	youthful ____
dignified ____	intelligent ____	pleasant ____	sensible ____	zestful ____
disciplined ____	intuitive ____	precise ____	sensitive ____	
dutiful ____	jovial ____	progressive ____	sentimental ____	
efficient ____	joyful ____	proud ____	serious ____	

This chart is adapted from a list by David W. Johnson in *Reaching Out: Interpersonal Effectiveness and Self-Actualization,* Sixth Edition. (Boston: Allyn and Bacon, 1997), pp. 60-62.

For Discussion/Reflection

To synthesize the preceding nine sessions as a group, think of several conflict situations of which the group is aware. Analyze each situation and discuss how it was treated. How would the skills that you have learned in this course help resolve the conflict?

Exercise 2

As a way of integrating what you have learned in the previous nine sessions, fill out the chart below. Discuss in smaller groups what new concepts you are most challenged by when working to communicate and to resolve conflicts.

Self-Assessment
Communication and Conflict Transformation Skills

	Rarely	Occasionally	Frequently	Usually
I am collaborative, confront conflict openly and fairly, and feel that conflict resolution is a method of growth.				
I use assertive responses effectively.				
I am honest with myself and with others about my feelings.				
I recognize and use the Assertive Bill of Rights and respect the rights of others to do the same.				
I paraphrase effectively in interpersonal communication.				
I am aware of the "Procedure for Resolving Interpersonal Disputes" and adapt it to situations that I'm involved with.				
I use the "Specific I Message."				
I ask for feedback when communicating my ideas.				
I recognize that others' views are valid.				
My nonverbal communication says the same thing that my verbal communication says.				
I am consciously aware of other people's nonverbal communication.				

Continue to develop the skills you learned in these sessions. Challenge yourself to improve the skills in the coming weeks as you encounter a variety of challenging interpersonal situations. Blessed are the peacemakers!

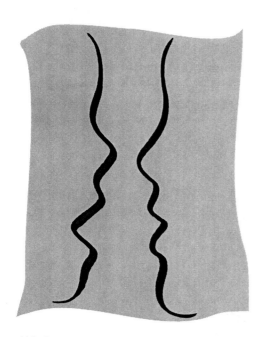

Appendix A
Agreeing and Disagreeing in Love

Commitments for Mennonites in Times of Disagreement

"**M**aking every effort to maintain the unity of the Spirit in the bond of peace" (Eph. 4:3), as both individual members and the body of Christ, we pledge that we shall:

In Thought

Accept conflict

1. Acknowledge together that conflict is a normal part of our life in the church. Romans 14:1-8, 10-12, 17-19; 15:1-7

Affirm hope

2. Affirm that as God walks with us in conflict we can work through to growth. Ephesians 4:15-16

Commit to prayer

3. Admit our needs and commit ourselves to pray for a mutually satisfactory solution (no prayers for my success or for the other to change but to find a joint way). James 5:16

In Action

Go to the other...

4. Go directly to those with whom we disagree; avoid behind-the-back criticism.* Matthew 5:23-24; 18:15-20

In the spirit of humility...

5. Go in gentleness, patience and humility. Place the problem between us at neither doorstep and own our part in the conflict instead of pointing out the others'. Galatians 6:1-5

Be quick to listen

6. Listen carefully, summarize and check out what is heard before responding. Seek as much to understand as to be understood. James 1:19; Proverbs 18:13

Be slow to judge

7. Suspend judgments, avoid labeling, end name calling, discard threats, and act in a nondefensive, nonreactive way. Romans 2:1-4; Galatians 5:22-26

Be willing to negotiate

8. Work through the disagreements constructively. Acts 15; Philippians 2:1-11

- Identify issues, interests, and needs of both (rather than take positions).
- Generate a variety of options for meeting both parties' needs (rather than defending one's own way).
- Evaluate options by how they meet the needs and satisfy the interests of all sides (not one side's values).
- Collaborate in working out a joint solution (so both sides gain, both grow and win).
- Cooperate with the emerging agreement (accept the possible, not demand your ideal).
- Reward each other for each step forward, toward agreement (celebrate mutuality).

In Life

Be steadfast in love

9. Be firm in our commitment to seek a mutual solution; be stubborn in holding to our common foundation in Christ; be steadfast in love. Colossians 3:12-15

Be open to mediation

10. Be open to accept skilled help. If we cannot reach agreement among ourselves, we will use those with gifts and training in mediation in the larger church. Philippians 4:1-3

Trust the community

11. We will trust the community and if we cannot reach agreement or experience reconciliation, we will turn the decision over to others in the congregation or from the broader church. Acts 15
    - In one-to-one or small group disputes, this may mean allowing others to arbitrate.
    - In congregational, conference district or denominational disputes, this may mean allowing others to arbitrate or implementing constitutional decision-making processes, insuring that they are done in the spirit of these guidelines, and abiding by whatever decision is made.

Be the Body of Christ

12. Believe in and rely on the solidarity of the Body of Christ and its commitment to peace and justice, rather than resort to the courts of law. 1 Corinthians 6:1-6*Go directly if you are European-North American; in other cultures disagreements are often addressed through a trusted go-between.

Adopted by the General Conference Mennonite Church Triannual Session and Mennonite Church General Assembly, Wichita, Kan., July 1995.

Appendix B
Bibliography

The following selections are from "Bibliography for Intermediary Roles and Practice II," a course Conflict Transformation Program, Eastern Mennonite University. Compiled by Ron Kraybill, June, 1997. Used with permission.

Group Facilitation, Group Problem-Solving, Group Decision Making

Bertcher, Harvey. *Group Participation: Techniques for Leaders and Members.* (Sage, 1979). An excellent source of ideas for specific techniques that leaders can use in working with groups, e.g., seeking and giving information, rewarding, responding to feelings, summarizing, and gatekeeping.

Fox, William M. *Effective Group Problem Solving* (San Francisco: Jossey-Bass, 1987). This book describes how to use the Improved Nominal Group Technique as a tool for group problem-solving. Written for business contexts, it is nevertheless applicable to groups in a variety of other settings.

Peck, M. Scott. *The Different Drum: Community Making and Peace* (Simon and Schuster, 1987). Reflections on the difficult task of building human community within groups. Peck traces out four stages that groups usually go through to reach genuine community: pseudocommunity, chaos, emptiness, and community. Easy-to-read, thought-provoking, includes some Christian theological reflection.

Schwarz, Roger M. *The Skilled Facilitator* (San Francisco: Jossey-Bass, 1994). Detailed examination of all aspects of group facilitation, from entry to diagnosis of problems to specific interventions to closure.

Tagliere, Daniel A. *How to Meet, Think and Work to Consensus* (San Diego, Calif: Pfeifer and Co., 1993). This book is written as a resource for team leaders in business or organizational settings. It is full of suggestions for accomplishing key tasks that teams typically face, such as communication within the team, constructive confrontation within the team, conducting team meetings, making decisions, creative problem-solving, making presentations to others. how to address specific problems.

Congregational Conflict

Cosgrove, Charles H. *Church Conflict: The Hidden Systems Behind the Fights.* Nashville: Abingdon Press, 1994.

Friedman, Edwin. *Generation to Generation: Family Process in Church and Synagogue.* New York: Guilford, 1985. Excellent in applying concepts of family systems' awareness to religious system.

Landis, Susan Mark. *Conflict in the Congregation: A Beginning Resource Guide for Congregational Leaders of the Ohio Conference of the Mennonite Church.* Kidron, Ohio: Ohio Conferences PJSC, 1994.

Leas, Speed. *Moving Your Church Through Conflict.* Washington, D.C.: Alban Institute, 1985. Provides an analytical framework for assessing the level of conflict and determining appropriate responses. This is an excellent resource by one of the most experienced church conflict intervenors around. It is likely to be especially appreciated by people seeking a clear conceptual framework.

Leas, Speed. *A Lay Person's Guide to Conflict Management.* Alban Institute, 1979. Thirteen pages of straightforward advice about what to do and what not to do in church conflict. Would make a useful reading assignment for people working in a church as an intervener.

McCollough, Charles R. *Resolving Conflict with Justice and Peace.* New York: Pilgrim Press, 1991.

Mennonite Conciliation Service. *Conflict in the Church: Division or Diversity?* Akron, Pa.: Mennonite Central Committee, 1988. A 12-minute video and discussion guide which examine the differences between a church "bound together by conflict" and another "divided by conflict." Useful tool in helping people who avoid conflict to take a more positive view of possibilities in conflict. Can be purchased or borrowed from MCC.

Mennonite Conciliation Service. *Mediation and Facilitation Training Manual: Foundations and Skills for Constructive Conflict Transformation.* 3d ed. Akron, Pa.: Mennonite Central Committee, 1995. This comprehensive manual draws on the accumulated experiences of a substantial number of Mennonite practitioners in dealing with conflicts in churches and community settings, and has substantial sections on group facilitation, decisionmaking, and conflict intervention. Packed with ideas, techniques, handouts, and many bibliographic suggestions. Probably the single best resource available in these areas.

Qualben, James D. *Peace in the Parish: How to Use Conflict Resolution Principles and Process.* San Antonio, Tex.: LangMarc Publishing, 1992.

Randall, Robert L. *Pastor and Parish: The Psychological Core of Ecclesiastical Conflicts.* New York: Human Sciences Press, 1988.

Steinke, Peter L. *How Your Church Family Works: Understanding Congregations as Emotional Systems.* (Washington, D.C.: Alban Institute, 1993.

Steinke, Peter L. *Healthy Congregations: A Systems Approach.* Bethesda, Md.: Alban Institute, 1996.

Thomas, Marlin. *Resolving Disputes in Christian Groups.* Winnipeg: Windflower Communications, 1994.

See also McKinney in the Group Facilitation section above.

Community, Environmental and Public Policy Processes

Carpenter, Susan L. and W.J.D. Kennedy. *Managing Public Disputes.* San Francisco: Jossey-Bass Publishers, 1988.

Creighton, James L. *Involving Citizens in Community Decision Making: A Guidebook.* Washington, DC: Program for Community Problem Solving, 1992. Makes the case for public participation in community issues and shows why lack of it often leads to polarization; lays out key steps in designing a public participation process; and describes a variety of techniques for use in involving people.

Crowfoot, James E. and Julia M. Wondolleck. *Environmental Disputes: Community Involvement in Conflict Resolution.* Washington, D.C.: Island Press, 1990. Seven case studies of mediation in environmental conflicts which give a good feel for the actual process.

Godschalk, David, et al. *Pulling Together: A Planning and Development Consensus-Building Manual.* Washington, D.C.: The Urban Land Institute, 1994. A how-to-do-it manual for building consensus among the varied interests effected by a decision or conflict in the public arena. Chapters on assessing the situation, designing the process, building consensus, solving problems, and running meetings. Also contains five case studies. Practical, clearly organized, no nonsense.

Jacksteit, Mary and Adrienne Kaufmann. *Finding Common Ground in the Abortion Conflict: A Manual.* Washington, D.C.: Search for Common Ground, 1995. Outlines a model for dialogue between opponents in the abortion debate; a model which could be easily adapted to other settings.

Maser, Chris. *Resolving Environmental Conflict.* Del Ray Beach, Fla.: St. Lucie Press, 1996.

McCoy, Martha, et al. *Planning Community-wide Study Circle Programs: A Step-by-Step Guide.* Pomfred, Conn. (Study Circles Resource Center), 1996. This is a guide for setting up "study circles" as a response to racism, but the concept could be used in any setting where there is tension and need for dialogue among a large number of people.

Schoene Jr., Lester and Marcelle E. DuPraw. *Facing Racial and Cultural Conflict: Tools for Rebuilding Community.* Washington, D.C.: Program for Community Problem-Solving, 1994.

Winer, Michael and Karen Ray. *Collaboration Handbook: Creating, Sustaining and Enjoying the Journey*. (St. Paul, Minn.: Amherst H. Wilder Foundation, 1994. This book is a richly woven tapestry of technical know-how, artful layout and diagrams, and stories, case studies, and wise sayings about building collaborative efforts among wary partners. It is mostly oriented towards building collaboration among community service organizations, but the basic ideas could easily be adapted to other settings.

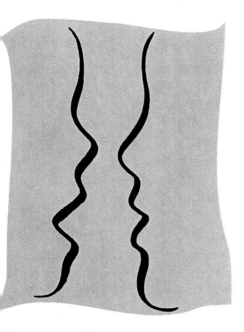

Leader's Guide

Although this booklet is structured around ten topics, it contains enough material to fill more sessions. Some topics will take more time than others. As the leader, you should determine ahead of time which topics are most relevant to your group, which ones need more time, and which might need be blended into one session.

Feel free to supplement the materials with your own experience, with the input of persons who have special experience in conflict resolution, or with input from participants based on their experience or research.

Purpose of This Curriculum

Since every person is unique, conflict and disagreements are inevitable. This curriculum was written to help people deal creatively with conflict by developing key communication skills.

Teaching Style

In leading the sessions, try to model the communication skills developed in this study. Use "I Messages" to state your feelings, paraphrase what participants say, draw out more discussion, and ask what people think of something you or the author says. Make participation a safe thing to do, so that people are free to express themselves. Invite disagreement and discussion, but model and expect that it be done in a productive, respectful way. Establish ground rules for class participation where necessary.

Format: In general, try to have each session include the following components:

1. **Your Own Preparation:** *Purpose:* Each session has a purpose, which is identified in sections below. Keep this in mind as you prepare the session.
Materials/Preparation: Prepare the classroom and gather the materials you will need before the group starts arriving.

2. **Introduction/Opening:** Open the session in a way that makes people feel welcome—with prayer, introductions, or in some other way that is inviting and comfortable.

3. Follow-Up: Allow time for follow-up questions and discussion based on the material from the previous session. Sometimes this will snowball, and you will need to cut it short. At other times you may want to generate discussion with starters like: What is the most important thing we discussed last week? What do you think of the statement from last week that [insert]?

4. Session Content: In general, follow the order of the study guide, unless another order makes more sense to you. You may want to add material of your own, or skip material that may not work for your group. The study guide includes the following types of material:

Text: Each session includes a few paragraphs on basic principles of conflict resolution and/or communication. Ask participants to read these before the session, summarize parts during the session, or read key portions aloud. Invite discussion about portions of text by using discussion starters like: Do you agree or disagree with what the author says here? Why? How would you summarize this section in one phrase or sentence? Sometimes the content will include the text of songs or Scriptures. Sing the songs, read the Scriptures, or supplement with similar resources that you gather.

Exercises: Most of these are designed for each participant to prepare written responses in their booklets. Some are group activities. Where possible, have participants do some of the exercises before the session, or leave some for participants to do on their own, if they are interested.

The exercises use situations from a variety of settings. Encourage participants to put themselves in the setting to do the exercise even if it is far removed from their current experience.

For Discussion/Reflection: There are usually a series of questions on the same theme where the discussion of the first questions forms the basis for later questions. Adapt these questions as you see fit; you may want to develop your own questions to further develop the theme for your context. It is not important to find answers to all of the questions in this section, but to use some or all of them to stimulate discussion and ideas.

5. Looking Ahead: The group learning experience will be deeper if everyone is committed to doing some reflection and preparation between sessions. Let participants know what to expect during the next session. Sometimes specific exercises are included at the end of the session material. Link the next session to a summary of the current session to show how it all fits together and builds a theme. Be sure to identify what you would like the participants to do even if you do not modify what the study guide says.

6. Closing: Close in a way that makes people glad they came.

7. Evaluation: After the session, ask yourself whether the purpose was accomplished. What main points were made during the session? Will the participants remember them? Use this evaluation to adjust how much time you allow for exercises and discussions in the coming sessions.

Session Helps

Chapter 1. Understanding Conflict

Purpose
To help each member of the group become aware of his or her normal response to conflict situations and begin thinking about how appropriate the various responses are.

Materials/Preparation
Study guide and pencil for each person, chalkboard, and chalk. Be sure you understand the scoring of the self-test and how it transfers to the chart.

Tips for Leading the Session
Introduction/Opening: In the first session, introduce yourself and welcome the participants to the group. Depending on how well participants know each other, do some activities to get to know each other better. Here are some ideas:

1. Divide the group into pairs who don't know each other well. Have the pairs talk for several minutes and then introduce each other to the group.

2. Write a few group conversation starters on the board and have each person complete the sentence(s) after giving his or her name. Group conversation starters are phrases like: "On Sunday afternoon I like to..." or "I come to this group because..."

After participants have introduced themselves, have the group brainstorm a list of examples of conflicts—from interpersonal to church to community to national to international. You may want to begin with some personal reflection time, in which participants write down (in the blanks provided) conflicts they have encountered. As an option, you may want to bring the front page of a newspaper for each person in the group. Use them to identify examples and levels of conflicts.

You could have participants identify what attracted them to this topic, and whether they have special areas that they would like to cover. Only do this if you are prepared to ensure that the topics identified are covered or to provide supplemental resources where people could look.

Exercise 1: This is a key component of this study, in which participants take the assessment and transfer the responses to the chart in the study guide. Stress that there are no correct answers and that participants will not be asked to share their responses with the group. Inevitably, participants will want to respond to the situations in ways different than those listed. Have them choose the two responses that are closest to the way they would respond. In transferring the responses to the chart, be sure to emphasize that lower and upper case letters stand for different responses.

Chapter 2. The Functions of Conflict

Purpose
To show that avoidance of conflict usually is not helpful and that people can work toward positive responses and results of conflict.

Materials/Preparation
Study guide and pencil for each person, chalkboard and chalk (or markers and flip chart), Bibles, a guitar or piano if you are planning to sing "Unity." Review dictionary definitions of and synonyms for "conflict" and "disagreement."

Tips for Leading the Session
Defining Conflict: In discussing this section, have the group brainstorm a list of words that describe conflict. List the words quickly, without evaluating the words. These almost always are negative words. Reflect with the group about why this is so.

Jesus' Response to Conflict: Here you may want to divide into smaller groups, each group taking a cluster of Scripture references and summarizing Jesus' response to conflict. Here is a summary of the stories:

> Matthew 19:16-30, Mark 10:17-31, and Luke 18:18-30 (Jesus' instructions to a rich man); Matthew 13:53-58, Mark 6:1-6, and Luke 4:16-30 (Jesus rejected at Nazareth because the people doubted his bold wisdom);
> John 10:22-42 (people rejected Jesus and were ready to stone him);
> Luke 4:16-30 and John 8:59, 10:39 and 11:45-57 (Jesus withdrew from situations);
> Mark 11:15-19 (Jesus overturned the tables of the money changers);
> Matthew 23:13-28, Mark 12:40, Luke 11:39-42, 44, 52, 20:47 (Jesus condemned hypocrisy); John 10:32 and 18:32 (Jesus defended himself).

Chapter 3. The Bible on Conflict

Purpose
To show that the Bible often advocates dealing with conflict rather than avoiding it.

Materials/Preparation
Study guide for each person, Bibles, and a guitar or piano if you are planning to sing "Many Gifts."

Tips for Leading the Session
Opening: Ask the group whether Chapters 1 and 2 cause participants to be more aware of conflict situations or of situation in which people avoided conflict in the past week.

Conflict Resolution in the Bible: Additional Scriptures to consider are: I Corinthians 1:10; Psalm 133:1; Romans 14:19; I Corinthians 6:1-6; Galatians 6:1; I Corinthians 12:4-31; Philippians 2:4; Romans 12:4-6a; Colossians 3:15; and Ephesians 5:29, 30.

Chapter 4. Honesty in Action

Purpose
To explore the appropriateness of being assertive, and to develop skills of assertiveness based on honesty.

Materials/Preparation
Study guide for each person, chalkboard and chalk (or markers and flip chart), Bibles, concordances.

Tips for Leading the Session

For the second discussion/reflection section (on responses to conflict), ask several participants ahead of time to share stories of how they have responded to conflict in submissive, aggressive or assertive ways. Be sensitive to those who are not prepared to be vulnerable in this way.

Exercise 2: You may do this in the session, or encourage people to do it on their own outside the session. If anyone in your group is not used to using a concordance, be sure to explain how to use one.

Chapter 5. Speaking Without Saying a Word

Purpose
To show the importance of nonverbal communication and explore how it can be used more effectively.

Materials/Preparation
Study guide and pencil for each person.
This session consists mainly of exercises. After doing an exercise, be sure to spend some time discussing the answers, results, reactions, and whatever else is appropriate.

Tips for Leading the Session
The topic of this Chapter lends itself to exercises. Here are a number of additional ideas that will involve some prior preparation:

1. Write out a script for a short play, and assign parts to the group participants. The script should include actions and emotions, but should have no spoken words. Have the group act out the nonverbal play, portraying its meaning as accurately as possible.

2. If the group includes people from different countries or cultures or with experiences in different cultures, discuss the differences in nonverbal communication between different cultures. What does this mean for dealing with conflict between members of different cultures?

3. Practice sending nonverbal messages with only facial expressions or solely without the use of facial expressions. Possibly conceal the parts of the body not used, and have others guess the message the person is trying to send. Do the same thing by looking at facial expressions in magazines, photo albums, or newspapers.

Chapter 6. What Did You Say?

Purpose
To increase communication skills by learning to listen actively and respond effectively.

Materials/Preparation
Study guide and pencil for each person.

Tips for Leading the Session

Introduction/Opening: Divide participants into groups of three. Tell each person to think of a story to tell. Have everyone tell the others the story at the same time. This will be very frustrating. Discuss how persons felt as they tried to tell something to others weren't listening.

Follow-Up: Discuss any observations relating to nonverbal communication that participants have made since last week. Were they more aware of nonverbal communication this past week? What did they notice?

Exercise 3: The correct associations are: 1. SAPI; 2. AIPS.

Optional Exercise: While the group takes notes, tell about an experience you've had. Then have someone in the group repeat the story. Discuss as a group what was left out or changed. Effective listening skills are essential in being able to repeat a story or statement that someone else tells.

Chapter 7. Speaking with Care

Purpose
To increase communication skills by developing speaking skills.

Materials/Preparation
Study guide and pencil for each person.

Tips for Leading the Session
Consider what Thomas Gordon, in *Parent Effectiveness Training* (New York: Peter H. Wyden, Inc., 1970, p. 117) calls an encoding and decoding process. For example, an older brother is approached by a younger brother to play or do something. The older brother is tired, and encodes this with the message "you are a pest." The younger brother hears this but decodes it as "I am bad." Thus, the message "I am tired" is translated into "I am bad." If the older brother had said "I am tired," the younger brother would have understood that "he is tired."

Chapter 8. What If the Other Person Is a Complete Idiot?

Purpose
To learn how to apply communication skills in situations in which the other person is not skilled in conflict resolution.

Materials/Preparation
Study guide for each person, guitar or piano if planning to sing "Prayer of St. Francis."

Tips for Leading the Session
At the heart of this lesson is the "Procedure for Discussing Interpersonal Conflict." This is one of the best tools to work at conflict in our lives. Make sure you plan enough time to work through the role-play exercises, so that the procedure "takes." Use an extra session if you need to.

Opening: Before the meeting, cut two identical sets of geometric figures out of construction paper. Each set should contain five or six different shapes. Do not mark the figures in any way. Have two people sit in chairs with their backs to each other, with a flat surface or desk in front of both. Give them each a set of the figures. Then have one of them make a design with the figures and describe it to the other, who tries to duplicate it with his or her set of identical figures. The second person cannot ask any questions of clarification or say any words whatsoever. When the first person is done describing the design, compare the designs. Discuss the communication dynamics. Was it effective? What impact did it have that the listener could not ask any questions? How did this affect the listener? How did it make the one describing the design feel?

Example of Dialogue: If possible, do this as a reader's theater.

Option: Ask participants to practice the "Procedure for Discussing Interpersonal Conflict" in a real conflict situation this week. It might be easier for them to initiate the discussion with their "partner" in conflict if they can say that this is an assignment. Ask the participants to be ready to report next week.

Closing: Sing the Prayer of St. Francis.

Chapter 9. The Third Party and Conflict

Purpose
To help participants understand the role of the third party in conflict resolution and explore the biblical call for the church to facilitate conflict resolution.

Materials/Preparation
Study guide and Bible for each person.

Tips for Leading the Session
This chapter is primarily an introduction to various kinds of third-party involvement in conflict management, not a study that will adequately train your participants as mediators, negotiators and arbitrators in complex conflicts. Try to stress in your session that for people to get involved formally in third-party intervention, they will probably need more training than this study can provide.

By this time in the study, you will probably have a sense of who in your group has gifts in mediation and the other forms of conflict resolution. Encourage them to pursue further training.

Opening: Ask participants to share how they were able to apply the "Procedure for Discussing Interpersonal Conflict" this week.

Issues That Determine: Note that these questions are listed as indications of the kinds of dilemmas faced by people engaging third parties in conflict. You may, however, use them as points of discussion in the group, or to help frame the input of guests you might invite (see next item).

Guests: Consider having one or more professionals involved in negotiation, mediation, arbitration, or litigation come to the group and describe their roles, experiences, perspectives, etc.

Chapter 10. Made in God's Image

Purpose
To help foster a healthy self-concept and to synthesize the previous nine chapters.

Materials/Preparation
Study guide and pencil for each person.

Tips for Leading the Session
To wrap up the study, you may want to choose either the material on healthy self-image, or the material that integrates the learnings of the previous sessions. Your choice may depend on how well the group has been synthesizing the material along the way. If it has done well with the material, it may want to focus more on a healthy self-image.

In any case, you may want to plan special closing activities for the study, such as refreshments, a time of prayer and commissioning, or some other ritual that sends participants on their way in practicing their communication skills.

Here are some additional exercises you may want to try in addition to, or instead of, the exercises in the study guide.

A Variation on Exercise 1: If members of the group know each other well, have each person write their name at the top of a piece of paper. Rotate the papers one to the right. Have each person write something positive about how the person whose name is at the top of the paper deals with conflict, and about his or her interpersonal communication skills. Then rotate the papers again, and keep repeating the process until each person receives his or her own paper back, filled with affirming statements about their skills developed in this group.

Self-Assessment Exercise Revisited: Go back to the Self-Assessment Exercise in Chapter 1 and apply conflict resolution skills and communication skills in developing appropriate responses to each of the situations.

Plan a Service: Have the group plan a worship service for your congregation based on the skills and messages in this group. Incorporate role plays, singing, reflection, discussion, and a variety of other activities. This could help the group solidify some of what it has learned, and could provide an educational experience for the congregation.

CPSIA information can be obtained at www.ICGtesting.com
Printed in the USA
267599BV00003B/27/P